Profitable Social Media Marketing

How To Grow Your Business By
Growing An Audience Using Facebook,
Twitter, Instagram, LinkedIn and More...

www.ExposureNinja.com
Free lifetime book updates at:
http://profitablesocialmediamarketing.com

Contents

Why Social Media?

Your mission (should you choose to accept) is to sell a pallet of the little glass jars shown below.

You can put candles in them, they look pretty and they're priced to be an impulse purchase. But the Internet is full of similar products and they've got a really broad target market. How do you get some attention for them?

You could run some Google ads. But with costs per click as high as £1.40 ($2), it's tough to justify the spend for such a low priced product.

You could try getting your website to the top of Google for the phrase "glass jars" but it'll take a long time and unless you're really committed, you might not get there.

Faced with this exact challenge, we decided to try something else. We contacted a popular blogger and offered her one set of glass jars (retailing at £12.50) as a prize for a reader competition. The competition was designed to take advantage of all the key elements of social media: people entered by liking, sharing and following our client's social channels; the blogger promoted it through her following on social media, and we piggybacked on the blog's authority and visibility to get attention for seller.

As entrants began liking and sharing the competition post, word began to spread and momentum built. Friends of friends started to get involved, and hundreds of Retweets began appearing on Twitter. Within one week the competition with a £12.50 prize had attracted a whopping 3,000 entries. Our client grew their Twitter following by 20%, generated hundreds of Tweets and Retweets, and asked how soon we could start the next giveaway.

To generate such buzz for such a low cost is very difficult with any other marketing channel. To get 3,000 positive responses for *anything* using traditional marketing is likely to cost a significant multiple of what an effective social campaign can cost. This book's goal is to help your business squeeze out every possible ounce of social media potential.

Most people in business fall somewhere between two extremes when it comes to social media:
On one side we have those who pledge allegiance to the flag of social media no matter what. They'll spend all day Tweeting, posting, sharing, hearting and whatever-else-ing because they love the interaction. To them it's not a business activity but a social activity and each notification is a piece of validation.

On the other extreme we have the stubborn skeptics. To them Twitter is for twits and LinkedIn is like dating for the under-employed. They refuse to dip their toes in the water for fear of being drowned in time vampire notifications and requests to be friends with people they spend their life trying to avoid.

The rest of us lie somewhere in between. Perhaps you've experimented with social media, but you're unsure how to integrate it with your marketing and daily activities, so it gets left behind. Or maybe you've heard how important social media can be, but without knowing where to start or what to aim for, it all seems a bit overwhelming.

Whether you're new to business or an experienced marketer looking to sharpen your saw with the new tools, this book will help you develop your own social media identity, incorporating the values that make your business special and giving you a roadmap for better social media visibility to grow your business.

We aim to prove that social media marketing doesn't just have to be about big brands with dedicated teams getting their topics trending. In fact it's actually the small and medium-sized businesses that have the most to gain from a well-designed social campaign. Learning lessons from the big brands and applying them to smaller businesses is the name of the game here. And of course we'll show you plenty of juicy home grown strategies we've developed managing the marketing for hundreds of businesses.

We'll also give you the ammunition to sell social media marketing to those in your organisation who might not share your enthusiasm or vision. They'll try to persuade you that it's a new fad, there's no ROI or that it's something that'll die out before long ("remember *MySpace?"* they'll ask).

The truth is that far from being a new fad, 'social marketing' is *the* oldest form of marketing.

Conversations between buyers of products and services have always been an important source of sales for businesses that offer something valuable and credible. In ancient times the cities along the Silk Road trade routes became culturally and economically rich because travellers shared their experiences, knowledge and wares. Today's social networks facilitate the same thing —- at the end of the day it's all just people talking about your business. The difference is that for the first time ever, these conversations are now happening in full view of a much bigger audience and within a few clicks of anyone who wants to find them.

Thanks to social, word of mouth can be measured, encouraged, promoted and even shaped in a more effective way than ever before. For the first time, savvy businesses can identify potential customers at their peak moment of need just because they *say* something. The future bride who Tweets a picture of her engagement ring should awaken every wedding dress shop in the local area to Tweet back their congratulations. This potential customer no longer needs to take the initiative — we can go to them and meet them where they are. Which is on their phone.

You and I can advertise to fans of a particular brand, product or lifestyle for just a few cents each, and in less than ten minutes. This has never happened before.

Even more significantly, we can build authority and attract a large targeted audience without paying a penny or leaving our seats. This opportunity is a different league to anything that's ever existed. Imagine what you had to do to build an audience of over ten million fans just fifteen years ago: hundreds of thousands in newspaper ads, PR, doing TV interviews, building a mailing list, travelling to seminars... YouTuber Adam Dahlberg's . Channel Skydoesminecraft has 11.5 million subscribers who regularly tune in to watch the 23-year-old play videogames from his desk. Where before has *that* been possible? The implication of this for every business is huge.

Critics of social media have completely missed this point, preferring to focus on the disposable and irrelevant aspects instead. They'll say things like "why would I use Twitter? I don't care what celebrities eat for breakfast". This is like saying "I don't read books because I'm not interested in trashy novels" or "I don't watch TV because I'm not interested in music videos". These critics focus on one tiny element of social media and disregard everything else. They're not only throwing the baby out with the bathwater, they're throwing the entire *bath* out as well. And besides, for many social media celebrities, that breakfast has positioning importance as well, but we'll come to that later.

Resistance is futile and those that refuse the advances of social media are similar to the businesses that failed to see how the early Internet was going to be important for anyone but the geeks who owned it. Ken Olsen (who surprisingly ran a computer company) famously said in 1977 "there is no reason for any individual to have a computer in his home". Those that dismiss Facebook as somewhere people go to watch cat videos are in very real danger of being the Ken Olsens of their generation.

With any revolutionary technology there will be two camps: the critics and those who recognise the potential and grab the opportunity with both hands.

Whether it's reaching more people than anyone else in your market; generating leads, or building your brand and positioning you and your business, social media *done properly* can be extremely profitable and genuinely transformational. And it doesn't have to have anything to do with photos of food and cats... unless you're a cat food company.

How Large Is The Opportunity?

The size of the potential audience is so big it's difficult to truly appreciate. Facebook's latest report puts the number of monthly active users at 1.49 *billion* people (that's double what it was in 2011). Twitter comes in at over 300 million. Instagram's 77 million users spend an average of twenty-one minutes per day using the app. That's 50% longer than they spend on mail, phone calls and email.

But what's *most* exciting is not the big numbers, as very few businesses will have something that a billion people want. What's much more exciting is that these big numbers are built from millions upon millions of different niches. Whether it's Chihuahua owners, Chihuahua puppy breeders or people who dress up as Chihuahuas at the weekend, if your audience shares a common interest, trait or goal, you can be in front of them within seconds. Wherever they live, whatever they spend their time doing and whichever magazines they read — they're all there using social media.

And it's not just consumer businesses. Social media channels have changed the way businesses interact with other businesses, potential investors and stakeholders as well.

Although all of this potential power can and should be used to your advantage, it can also bring negative attention. Whilst many large brands have dedicated social media teams, they still don't know what to do when someone starts kicking off. Now that customers can (and do) head straight to Twitter or Facebook to complain or praise any aspect of a business, how does the smart company react? Many brands choose to ignore it, hoping it will go away. They're scared of being held to ransom by angry customers with influence on social networks. But as we'll see later in the book, trying to ignore social is a wasted opportunity to sell more.

If you're reading this book it's unlikely that you need to be sold on the opportunity that social media presents. Perhaps you've identified that your market has an opportunity for a truly social business to stand out.

At Exposure Ninja, we spend all day working and talking with a range of businesses on the frontline. It's very rare — almost unheard of — that we'll see a market with more than a couple of players using social media *really* effectively. Whether it's a lack of resources or an unwillingness to take the risk, your competitors are almost certainly underusing social so it's up to you to figure out a path that helps you grow. Don't wait for things to be perfect before you start, and remember: in the land of the blind, the one eyed man is king. Any time you are doing something better than your competitors, keep doing it. Your efforts in social media could well be the most important thing you do for your business this decade.

Free Gifts

Before we get started, we want to say a big thank you for buying this book and for helping to make it one of the world's bestselling Social Media titles.

To say thanks, we'd like to help you grow your business totally free of charge.

Gift 1. The World's Most Useful Marketing Review

Curious to see what some of the world's smartest marketers would do to blow up your visibility online?

Visit www.profitablesocialmediamarketing.com now, pop your details in the quick form and one of our expert team will carry out analysis of your existing marketing, including social media, and outline a step-by-step strategic plan to help you get you in front of more people and sell more. It's completely free and there's no catch. We'll even show you what your competitors are doing, and identify any opportunities that they're missing.

Over 4,000 businesses have benefited from this review, and many have grown significantly as a result of taking the advice we gave them free of charge.

Gift 2. Free Lifetime Book Updates

Because the world of social media changes so frequently, we're constantly updating this book. In order to keep you up-to-date with the very latest techniques and strategies, we'd like to offer you free lifetime book updates.

Each time the book is updated, you'll receive an email summarising the changes, as well as the full new edition.

Head to www.profitablesocialmediamarketing.com to claim your lifetime updates now.

Gift 3. Free Getting Started On Social Video Series

Lastly if you'd like a free video series that takes you step-by-step through the process of setting up your campaign, head over to www.profitablesocialmediamarketing.com and fill in the necessary form.

Why Did We Write This Book?

This book is written for those who, like us, believe that social media is a marketing activity, and any marketing activity should have a return on investment.

Whether you're a large brand social media manager or a startup entrepreneur on late nights, early mornings and caffeine, the most important word in the title of this book is 'profitable'. Marketing activity that isn't ultimately focused on profit is a waste of time. Startups don't have the time or resources for anything that doesn't grow the business and, come to think of it, large companies don't either.

Our clients are usually small and medium-sized companies, with the odd multinational corporation thrown in to remind us what a bad idea decision by committee is. From local plumbers and boutiques, large e-commerce stores and manufacturing businesses, to household names like DHL, we do everything required to get our clients more business from the Internet. We started off building websites, getting them ranked on Google and running paid advertising. As the Internet has evolved, social media has become more and more important. Two years ago businesses could get away without social media. In 2016, it's possible to build an entire business *purely* through Ninja social media.

Whilst we have a number of bestselling books, we'll always be 'doers' rather than authors. We wrote this book ourselves so there are bound to be places where the grammar ain't quite right. We might start sentences with the words 'and' and 'but'. And we might write how we talk. But hopefully that doesn't distract from the message, and the ideas that you generate as you read.

Feedback and Comments Welcome!

I really hope you enjoy reading this book as much as I have enjoyed putting it together for you. If you have any comments, suggestions or feedback you can contact me directly tim@exposureninja.com

If you're not happy with the book in any way, I'd also like to know. I'd be happy to personally refund you the cost of the book if you don't consider it a good investment. Just drop me an email and we'll get it sorted :-)

Tim Kitchen
December 2015

What Ninja Social Media Looks Like

Although in this book we're primarily interested in 'real' business social media (i.e. we don't have Coca-Cola's budget or Apple's brand loyalty... yet), it can be useful to look at how large brands use social, their successes and failures and the commonalities that link them.

Let's have a look first at some successes, and see if we can draw out what made the difference:

Air Asia 'Plane Giveaway'

When Air Asia opened a new flight route between Sydney and Kuala Lumpur, it wanted a way to get publicity, particularly amongst potential customers living nearby. It also had a shiny new range of Airbus A330 planes that it wanted to show off.

Rather than running pages of expensive display ads in magazines, Air Asia headed to Facebook and offered to give away an entire plane to one lucky winner. This person could choose their 302 closest friends to join them on a free flight along the new route.

Visitors to the Facebook page were shown a virtual tour of the new aircraft, and were then asked to choose which of their Facebook friends would be joining them on the flight. The final step in the contest was where the magic happened, as entrants were invited to identify their top fifty friends who would receive notification that they had been entered into the contest. Imagine logging in to Facebook and seeing that you've been chosen as one of fifty closest friends to get a free private flight on an aeroplane. No matter how busy you are, you're probably going to check that notification.

And people did. Within two days of going live, the campaign had attracted 4,000 entries and went on to grow Air Asia's fan page by 22,000. In total the campaign reached over 2.2 million people — 20% of Australian Facebook users. The publicity it generated wasn't too shabby either.

There are two things that we like about this campaign that any business, no matter their budget, can use:

Firstly the prize was relevant to the intended target audience. A trip from Sydney to Kuala Lumpur is *exactly* what they were promoting, and by using it as a prize, competition entrants self-selected as potential customers. A new route between Sydney and Kuala Lumpur is of no interest to someone living in Alaska, but that's OK — those guys won't bother entering. Air Asia wanted Sydney residents to tag all their Sydney-based friends, who will enter and tag *their* Sydney-based friends. So the prize attracted *relevant* traffic.

The second takeaway is how they built sharing into the entry process. The prize was sufficiently desirable and exciting that entrants' friends were unlikely to feel

20

'bugged' by having been invited. The number of shares encouraged (fifty per entry) meant that the viral spread was huge.

Old Spice Guy

Things weren't so great at Old Spice in 2009. Facing declining sales and seen as completely irrelevant by a lot of young people, they needed to turn things around with the promotion a new body wash range. Marketing agency Wieden+Kennedy identified a message that few of its competitors could match:

"A big question for us at the time was the name and whether the brand could be relevant to young men moving forward. An early and key decision was to turn this perceived weakness into a strength. With its 70-year brand heritage Old Spice was 'experienced' and well positioned to be an expert on masculinity and being a man." — Jess Monsey, W+K

They also spotted that women made more than 50% of men's body wash purchases, so the social media voice would need to appeal to both sexes if it was going to be effective.

They built the character 'Old Spice Guy'. Old Spice Guy demonstrated that if only your man stopped using ladies' body wash, he'd be more muscular, give you diamonds and buy you tickets "for that thing you like". He confidently (but with his muscular tongue in his cheek) spoke to the camera about what it was like being "the man your man could smell like". The message and execution was perfect, and the video went viral.

The marketing team noticed that the video generated a huge response on YouTube, so they set about creating a follow up that could capitalise on this viral element. They decided to run a 2-day campaign where Old Spice Guy would respond to audience questions by posting video answers, almost in real time.

They got a camera, a teleprompter, three scriptwriters, and started 'listening' across all social media platforms for questions. When questions came in, they filmed video answers as quickly as they could. Writers fed the scripts to Old Spice Guy on a teleprompter and he read them out live on camera.

To boost the visibility of the campaign early on in the first day, Old Spice Guy answered questions from celebrities such as Ellen Degeneres and Perez Hilton. The team knew that these influencers wouldn't be able to resist sharing the videos with their followers, and the campaign would pick up viral momentum.

The videos attracted 65 million views and made Old Spice the most popular brand channel on YouTube. The campaign also grew their Twitter following 2,700% and their Facebook audience by 800%. Sales increased year on year 125% and made Old Spice body wash the top seller in America.

The main takeaway here is that by identifying an angle for their business that was new, funny and entertaining, they managed to turn body wash for 'old men' into one of the biggest viral campaigns in history.

Rather than building in sharing, they used one-on-one communication and humour to ensure that the audience would share on their own accord. It was a perfect message to market fit, well executed and extremely profitable.

Cadbury's One Million Fans

Cadbury was an early adopter of social media and viral advertising and in 2012 started one of its most interesting marketing campaigns, resulting in an additional 40,000 new fans for its Facebook page.

When their Facebook fan count reached one million, Cadbury decided to celebrate by building a giant Facebook 'like' thumb out of pieces of Dairy Milk chocolate.

They used teaser ads to build up anticipation, then once the thumb was ready the team live streamed it from a studio decorated with user-generated content and photos. The Cadbury team was on hand to respond to user requests and comments in the video. In total, over 350,000 people were actively involved in the campaign.

That's 350,000 people who now have a deeper association with Cadbury than any other chocolate brand, and who took time out of their day to interact and receive the marketing message.

This campaign worked because people are curious about anything big or unusual. If you can do something sufficiently big or sufficiently kooky, people *will* take notice.

Dumb Ways to Die

Inventive social media campaigns don't have to focus purely on driving sales of products. Causes and charities are just as well (if not better) placed to benefit from a savvy strategy.

Australian train company Metro wanted to raise awareness about rail safety. The challenge they faced was that nobody really wants to watch a video about something as boring as rail safety.

So instead of running dull, preachy newspaper ads, they came up with a funny video (and catchy theme song) called 'Dumb Ways To Die'. In the video, animated characters illustrate funny and increasingly stupid ways to be killed, from sticking a knife into a toaster to pressing a big red button without knowing what it blows up. The message comes at the end, as the last deaths in the video are caused by characters standing too close to the platform edge, running across railway rails and driving around crossing barriers.

The message Metro Transport wanted to promote was seen by 113 million people as the video went viral. On the back of this success, the team released an app and website www.dumbwaystodie.com, complete with a shop where fans can buy the characters featured in the video.

But aside from spawning a merchandising empire that seemed to turn Metro trains into a sort of morbid Aussie Disney, did the campaign actually achieve its goal of raising railway awareness?

Well apparently the answer is yes. According to Metro it contributed to a 30% reduction in 'near miss' accidents.

As a side note the video was banned by the Russian government over fears that it encouraged viewers to kill themselves and provided them a list (complete with illustrated instructions) of exactly how to do it.

When social campaigns like these take off, the reach that they attract can be far more significant than what would be possible for the same budget using traditional media. Imagine the cost of TV ads to tell 113 Million people not to drive around railway crossing barriers, or the campaign required to make Old Spice Guy a household name *without* the use of social media.

When It All Goes Wrong

But we've also seen some big brand social media disasters where the marketing team failed to get the message right, or inadvertently attracted a hostile audience with poor execution. Imagine being in charge of some of these...

McDstories

In the hope of triggering nostalgic thoughts of happy McDonald's-based memories, their social media team created the hashtag "#McDstories".

Rather than representing fast and simple food, the McMarketers hoped that this hashtag would get people thinking and talking about their memories of good times and happy meals shared with friends and family at McDonald's. Instead this optimistic little hashtag turned into an ugly viral nightmare when people started sharing horror stories and gripes about service, food, hygiene and anything else negative about McDonald's.

The McDonalds social media team had to sit back and watch as the Twittersphere exploded with Tweets like:

"Eating a Quarter Pounder value meal makes me feel exactly the same as an hour of violent weeping. #McDStories" - @mmemordant

And

"My father used to bring us McDonald's as a reward when we were kids. Now he's horribly obese and has diabetes. Lesson learned. #McDStories" - @natebramble

The crucial mistake Ronald and co made here was that they expected their fans to be passionate enough about McDonald's to use the hashtag positively, but actually a large portion of the *true* passion surrounding McDonald's is negative. By leaving the hashtag so open to interpretation, they were asking for trouble. As soon as influencers started picking up on the backlash, the negativity itself went viral. As more people piled in hijacking the hashtag (which had now earned the title 'bashtag'), they began using it to share their own

27

humour and witty Tweets. Viral works both ways and it's not easy to stop once it starts.

The McDonald's team didn't really have a response and although the campaign ran out of steam eventually, it's memorialised forever now in this book as a social media fail.

American Apparel During Hurricane Sandy

Capitalising on current news stories can be risky business even when you have the best of intentions, and American Apparel makes our 'DO NOT GO THERE' list for their horrendously ill-advised Hurricane Sandy campaign.

The clothing brand decided to offer a 20% discount during the hurricane, already risking accusations of opportunism. But their message, "In case you're bored during the storm, get 20% off for the next 36 hours" wasn't very well received by the American customers huddled in basements waiting for the second costliest hurricane in American history to destroy their homes.

#WaitroseReasons

High-end UK supermarket chain Waitrose ran their own hashtag campaign, which started to turn sour in a similar way to #McDStories. But their handling of what happened when hashtags go wild serves as a useful lesson in reputation management.

The campaign started when Waitrose decided to ask their followers to complete this sentence: "I shop at Waitrose because _____. #WaitroseReasons". No doubt they wanted their customers to talk about the quality of the produce, the great shopping experience and anything else that made them feel just that little bit more special by shopping at Waitrose.

But the replies they received were not quite along the lines they hoped. People mocked the brand and made fun of the 'posh' image. For example, Polly Courtney Tweeted:

"I shop at Waitrose because Clarissa's pony just *WILL NOT* eat ASDA value straw. #WaitroseReasons"

While @Amoozbouche wrote

"I shop at Waitrose because it makes me feel important and I absolutely detest being surrounded by poor people #waitrosereasons"

This single Tweet was Retweeted 127 times. #waitrosereasons had gone bad viral.

To their credit, rather than shy away or remove their own Tweets, Waitrose took the responses in good humour and thanked the audience for making them smile. By not getting too defensive they diffused the situation and showed a human side.

Starbucks #SpreadTheCheer

Starbucks generally gets a lot of love for their social media use, but their presence in our fail list shows that nobody gets it right *all* the time. In 2012 they were widely criticized in the UK for their tax practices, after it was revealed just how little corporation tax they pay despite their large turnover. Some of this public resentment started spilling out into their social media interactions.

At the height of the negative publicity around Christmas 2012, they decided to run an ill-advised Christmas PR campaign with the hashtag #SpreadtheCheer. As if that wasn't skating on thin enough ice, they decided to display the resulting messages on a large screen in the Natural History museum for all to see. You guessed it...another hashtag disaster.

"I like buying coffee that tastes nice from a shop that pays tax. So I avoid @starbucks #spreadthecheer" - @dickdotcom

@SpatchcockOfTheYard pitched in: "Tax paid: £8.6m. Additional tax paid to improve public image: £20m. Posting live Tweets to a big screen: priceless.#spreadthecheer"

While other Tweeters used the hashtag as an opportunity to air separate grievances:

"Starbucks' anti labor behaviors mean my good friend has to work three 12 hour shifts two days after giving birth.#spreadthecheer" - @ashponders

The lesson? Ask for people to air their opinions only when you know that on the whole their opinions are going to be positive. Feedback in business is priceless, but you don't want an unhappy audience leading the conversation about your brand on social media.

These companies could have avoided their social media disasters by observing what people are currently saying about their brands *before* starting a campaign. Address these grievances first, before you ask people to broadcast them in full public view.

Although examples like these generate a ton of negative publicity, they demonstrate just how involved people can become in social campaigns. Don't look at these and get too scared to try your own. Look at these and get excited that there's a medium out there that can generate such a significant response for those who use it well.

Although these campaigns all feature large companies, the lessons, strategies and underlying principles remain the same for businesses of any size. The smart response to these case studies is not "that strategy would never work for my business" but "*how* can I use that strategy in my business?"

How To Create an Epic Social Media Marketing Strategy in 5 Steps

Before even dipping your toes into the social world, it is smart to plan out a strategy that can be used to grow your business. Yes, social media can be fun but it also can have a very measurable impact on the bottom line. Let's go through the process of planning a strategy for your business

Step 1: What's The Goal?

The first step to any successful social campaign is identifying your end goals. You might be facing challenges such as: is your customer loyalty low? Has you traffic dipped? Do you feel that you're missing out on potential customers due to low social visibility? Having a clear map before you set off greatly increases your chances of arriving somewhere profitable, and most successful campaigns have clear goals in place from the start. Let's take a look at some social media goals:

End Goal #1: Social Selling

Direct response (or 'DR') is the most straightforward and measurable form of advertising around: show something to a prospect, ask them to buy, get a 'yes'. There are various ways to make sales directly through social media, but in general it's a good idea to avoid coming across too 'sales-y', as that can quickly turn your audience off.

Social selling is defined as the process of forging relationships through social channels, in order to sell more. It's about creating trust with your customers, similar to the type of trust they would have when asking their friends or family for recommendations about a product. Although selling *directly* through social media is usually most effective for e-commerce businesses sitting in a passion-fuelled niche, such as music, art, hobbies and sports, forging these relationships and creating this type of trust with customers helps any business, no matter their market.

Musicians can send their fans directly to their online shop on release day to grab new music or merchandise. Authors sharing the Amazon page for their newly released book will have a similar success if their audience is already warm and rapport is strong. Some fashion and beauty e-commerce sites can use a direct sales approach too, because their audience loves their style to the extent that they're more than happy to flick through their product ads in their social feed.

For a real life example, check out https://www.facebook.com/Earthegy. Their relentless pitching might appear tiresome to people that aren't into gemstone jewelry, but through the implementation of smart social selling (nailing the message for their audience), founder Chrisy has built the page to over 115,000 fans with a reasonably high level of engagement. If a business with lower affinity tried this (think supermarket, general online store), engagement would be low and post visibility would be rock bottom.

There are three keys to social selling: **research, authenticity** and **lead nurturing**. The **research** is about understanding and profiling your ideal customer, which we'll be looking at shortly. Picking your audience means you can laser target your message, and write/choose content to share in a way that feels **authentic** to your audience. This is actually much trickier than it sounds, because the tendency is to hide behind a particular type of corporate voice, or copy other brands that have a DNA, but that's not what works on social. The most successful social pages often have a voice that comes across like a genuine and authentic *individual*. To develop this authentic personality, we first need to find some common ground and use it as an entry point to establish a conversation that will later turn into a "friendship".

Friendship bonds take time to develop, and that's where the **nurturing** element comes in. If you think back to the strongest friendships you've developed in your life, there was usually a period of 'courtship', with shared experiences leading to realisations that you thought in a similar way. This is what we want to mimic on social. Just because someone clicked on your Facebook ad, visited your website or even liked you Facebook, that doesn't mean that they are ready to purchase. You wouldn't try to sell a new sales prospect something immediately without building a relationship first, let alone someone you were trying to build a friendship with.

Even if you think that your audience will be responsive to constant sales messages, care should be taken to balance these with entertaining and informative content, blog posts, videos and the sort of stuff that people are on social media for in the first place. You might have noticed that if your posts don't get much engagement on Facebook (likes, comments, shares and clicks) they start losing visibility. Pages that are entirely self-promotional risk getting caught in this vicious cycle: their posts get no attention so they create more posts. When these don't get attention either, they continue the same strategy until Facebook barely shows them any more. In our experience this is the main challenge facing most small business Facebook pages.

Of course the idea of being able to sell straight from Tweets and posts can seem appealing. After all, social media can be mistaken for free advertising, leading some business owners to keep posting their new

36

products over and over again. The danger comes when the business starts to believe that their audience's goal is to buy more products: it's not. Any audience is always asking "'what's in it for me?" and the answer is not that they really want more product pitches in their social feeds.

Bournemouth Pizza Co is a small startup pizza restaurant that used social selling very sensitively to build their following online when the restaurant first opened. They made their Facebook special offers only visible on Facebook, so customers have to mention that they saw the offer on the Facebook page in order to get the special price or the free side. This gives their Facebook fans the feeling that they are insiders, but it also tells the restaurant staff how effective their social media campaigns are, because each Facebook-generated customer is clearly identifying himself or herself at the point of sale. To keep growing their Facebook fan base, they promoted the page in store so that customers sat waiting for their pizza, smartphone in hand, could start checking out the offers. They click 'like' and they're now part of the "family" — set to receive marketing messages and offers, increasing the chance of a repeat visit.

The most effective social media pages balance the sales approach by mixing in the sort of entertaining and interesting content people actually go to Facebook, Twitter and Instagram for in the first place.

Fitness Supplement Company Shredz built their entire brand from scratch on Instagram using the right mixture of sales and entertainment. People use Instagram because they enjoy spending their time looking at things they like, whether that's DIY craft ideas, cars and homes, or the everyday lives of people they like or admire. In Shredz' case, their audience enjoys looking at pictures of fitness models and their lifestyles.

The 1.6 million followers on https://instagram.com/shredz see a mixture of fitness pictures, recipes, workout gear and, of course, sales pitches for Shredz supplements. Some of these are overt, such as special offers and discounts exclusively for followers, but many are subtler. Before and after pictures from Shredz customers serve as motivation for the audience, but also tell a story that sells more product. Images of Shredz sponsored athletes working out in the gym with their Shredz supplements neatly stacked next to them reinforces the association between Shredz and living the lifestyle their target market aspires to. And it works: revenue went from $90,000 in the company's first year to $5 million in year two.

But social selling doesn't stop there. To expand their reach further, Shredz athletes are given their own online stores with voucher codes that *their* followers can use to get discounts on Shredz supplements, and the athletes earn a nice commission from doing so. The end result is that a significant proportion of the most successful fitness profiles on Instagram are mixing their content with Shredz adverts (both overtly and subtly) and the brand is exploding as a result.

End Goal #2: Loyalty and Retention

According to the Chartered Institute of Marketing, it can cost between five to eight times more to attract a new customer than it does to keep an existing one.[1] By getting existing customers to follow you on social and constantly drip-feeding useful and helpful content to them, you can stay at the front of their mind until the buying cycle repeats and they're in the market for their next purchase.

The three main methods you can use to increase loyalty are:
1. Give your fans a voice. By Retweeting or sharing positive feedback, you're giving a very public pat on the back to those that praise you. This reward elicits more of the same behaviour

---

[1] http://www.camfoundation.com/PDF/Cost-of-customer-acquisition-vs-customer-retention.pdf

and for some brands has become a significant portion of their social content. Fashion e-commerce site Missguided (@missguided) regularly Tweets pictures of their customers wearing their clothing, and inviting their audience to heap on praise. Fans have built up such a personal relationship with the persona of the business that they post videos of their 'Missguided Hauls' (that's what they call huge orders) on YouTube.

2. Address public questions or concerns. A great example is LOFT, a clothing brand owned by Ann Taylor Inc., who received immense backlash on their Facebook page after posting a photo of a slim female modeling clothes from their new collection. Their target audience, real women, spoke out against the picture. But instead of staying silent, LOFT addressed this customer concern publicly by posting an album of actual staff members posing with their favourite LOFT pieces. Real women modeling real clothes. People understand that brands are run by people, who make mistakes. However, how the brand decides to deal with the mistake can certainly strengthen customer brand loyalty and prompt retention. Other examples include exceptional customer service (like JetBlue Airways that are extremely responsive to their clients and/or Nike, which has a separate

Twitter account @NikeSupport to address customer problems.

3. Reinforce the benefits of your product or service by showing it in action and continually posting reminders of why your customers bought from you. With the average car buying cycle being around four years, vehicle manufacturers can use social media to gently remind their fans about new models, key benefits and the brand's tone of voice (positioning). Rather than sitting and waiting for four years dismissing those who recently bought a car as untargeted prospects, the car companies are effectively loading prospects straight back into the start of the funnel for the next purchase. This approach works — an AddThis study found that 15% of vehicle buyers were influenced by social media in their purchase decision.

With some skillful positioning and cultivated word of mouth, you can use your existing customer base to find some new-targeted customers through social referrals. Asking for Facebook or Google+ reviews not only builds the strength of your social 'pitch', but also exposes you to the friends and followers of the happy customer, who can now see this public recognition. Nielsen found that 92% of people trust referrals from those they knew, and 91% of customers are willing to give a referral. The Missguided Hauls that bloggers post about are essentially referrals to Missguided, fuelled by their love and passion for the brand's social personality.

Once someone has bought from you they have the potential to become an extremely effective walking, talking, Tweeting/Instagramming/Snapchatting/Face booking advertisement. But very few people will do this out of their own initiative, so we need to make sure that there's a definite process in place.

1. Each of your followers is considered an authority by their audience. Just because they only have twenty-five followers, doesn't mean they aren't important. The most important thing that a business should look for when looking at customers audiences is not the amount of followers they have, but the interaction. The question is not: *how many followers do they have?* It is: *do people interact, Retweet, comment, share with this person?* A recommendation they make to their audience is more believable than anything you could say about your own business because of who is making it.

2. People Retweet and share things for a number of reasons, but very rarely through wanting to help you out or simply 'spread the word' (unless you have built a ridiculously compliant audience). Whether it's to appear as an insider

with access to exclusive information, to get a real reward (discount, gift or voucher) or because their association with you boosts their own self-image, it's important to understand which of these drives you are tapping into. Remember that everybody acts from a place of self-interest, so there has to be something in it for them, even if it's a feeling of significance.

3. Many markets contain tastemakers — authorities on all that is new and good. People who see themselves as tastemakers will seek out and promote causes, organisations and businesses that they feel match their criteria and enhance their position by sharing. For example each town has its 'foodies' who like the feeling of discovering and championing a new great place to eat. Rather than doing this purely from a 'spreading the word' standpoint, they are doing this to increase their positioning as a tastemaker and source of knowledge. If a tastemaker has enough authority, their approval can be a huge boost to the visibility and exposure of your business. Like fitness clothing companies sending merchandise to influential fitness bloggers on Instagram and Pinterest, there is likely to be something you can do to attract the attention and goodwill of these tastemakers. It's important to understand the mindset of the tastemaker though, and allow them the feeling of 'discovering' you. By all

43

means send free stuff, but don't pitch it too hard
or they'll feel like you are trying to control them,
and that's like kryptonite to someone who has
built up their own brand by providing trustworthy
personal recommendations.

Social referrals have been central to the viral growth of
companies like Dropbox, Airbnb and Uber. Whilst
signing up for these services, users are offered the
chance to refer friends via Facebook to earn free
storage, money and Uber rides. Meanwhile lingerie
company True&Co offers users $15 off their purchases
for referrals, and even provides you a unique referral
link that you can post to your social feeds. Anyone that
makes a purchase from this link also qualifies you for
your referral voucher. If you want to try setting this up
yourself, Referral Candy
(http://www.referralcandy.com) is a cheap way to get
started without having to develop your own custom
solution.

You'll notice that most successful social referral
campaigns build the referral request right into the
signup process, in order to hit the visitor right when
they're at their peak engagement.

End Goal #3: Awareness

A trap that many new marketers fall into is thinking of
everybody using Facebook, Twitter or Instagram as a
single audience. If social media is a sea, they think of

their marketing campaign as a very wide net. They lob it in and hope that it'll pick up the right sort of fish for the dish they're cooking tonight. The trouble is that wide nets are expensive and pick up a lot of crap. Businesses casting a wide social media net are much better off when they find where the right fish hang out, throw in some targeted bait, and pick out loads of the *right* type of fish.

Thanks to audience targeting on every social network, finding the right fish for your business is usually pretty straightforward. If your audience is sports fans for example, let's run some ads targeting those that like a particular football club. If you need sports fans that drive new-ish Range Rovers, with a university education, living in Spain, you're in luck. Almost without exception every target audience is out there, it's just a case of narrowing down your search and understanding the identifying traits of your perfect customer. Later on we'll look at how the social networks themselves (Facebook in particular) will help us profile our most responsive customers.

Awareness is most often a goal for businesses that have a specific audience but who might not be ready to buy right now. New businesses usually need to raise awareness amongst their target audience, whether it's to attract funding or kick start sales. In this situation, having established competitors can give you a distinct advantage, as you can piggyback the audience they've already spent money building.

Launching a hotel? Let's do some outreach to followers of existing hotels in your city. Promoting a furniture e-commerce store? Let's find people that like established furniture stores selling a similar sort of product, or manufacturers of those products. The established players have already done the work of collecting an audience, and there's nothing that stops you sneaking in and advertising to them.

If you don't have established competitors, that's usually good news too because it means your audience is being underserved. In the short term it means you'll have to work a little harder to collect your target customers together in the first place, but once you have them they'll be receptive.

Step 2: Research, Listen and Compare

There is a lot that needs to be done before a business clicks the "Tweet" or "publish" button. The idea is to create a solid plan before even starting to use social channels so that social media efforts will not fall on deaf ears or even worse the wrong type of ears.

The first thing that needs to be established is: *who will you be talking to?* And one of the best ways to do this is by creating a customer persona. Customer personas

46

are fictional representations of your ideal customers that are based on data and interviews and supported by educated speculation. So how do we create a customer persona? First, to understand your customers' unique characteristics and behaviors, businesses must segment their audience. Audience segmentation is a process that divides people into subgroups based upon certain criterion like media use and/or demographics. There are three main types of segmentation: demographic, behavioral and attitudinal. Second, business must determine what problems their product solves and think about the type of person that might want to use this product/service.

Some of the types of questions that you should pose when determining customer characteristics can include:

1. How old are they?
2. Where are they located?
3. Are they mostly men or women?
4. How do we present this type of product to these individuals
5. Where do they get their information - through social media, online news and/or traditional media?

6. What type of content works best (check with competitors)? Video? Still images? Custom graphics? Written content?

Demographics and geography are vital statistics of your customer base. Demographics can cover things like age, level of education, job classification, income, marital status and ethnic background. Beyond demographics, businesses can also focus on psychographics that refer to personality and emotional behaviors that influence the customer's purchases. In short, what are the buying habits of your customer? Lastly beliefs and lifestyle (particularly they way consumers look at themselves) could prove beneficial as they may predict future purchasing behavior. The idea is not only to create the ideal customer, but to consider their motivations behind them purchasing your product and/or service.

To gather this type of information businesses should also try to listen to what their customers have to say. This can be done in a number of ways, such as organising focus groups and/or other types of initiatives in an effort to talk to and learn from their customers. Lastly, bring your persona to life with a photo and a name! Make sure to summarise all the information you collected in a short document that you could later refer to when planning your marketing strategies. In the end, your customer persona should impact what you can and should be doing on social media.

Below is an example of a customer/buyer persona provided by Shopify:

ALEX

Lives In: Canada, United States

Age: 25 - 40

Gender: Male

Interests: Fitness and Wellness, Shopping and Fashion, Sports and Outdoors, Technology

Education Level: College Graduate

Job Title: Finance, Financial Advisor, Financial Analyst or Financial Adviser

Income: 45k-75k

Relationship Status: Single

Interested In: Women

Language Spoken: English

Buying Motivation:
Wants to stand out in a boring workplace.

Buying Concerns:
Alex is price conscious and responds well to sales and discounts.

Another step is to analyse and check with competitors and their social media pages to see what works best and make even learn from their mistakes. Vibhu took six steps from Avinash Kaushik's 10 best practices on the Occam's Razor blog to compile his competitor analysis checklist. Some of the interesting points to note include:

1. Visit the website and note the objectives and what has worked and what might not have worked
2. Note the acquisition strategy — analyse their traffic sources, such as organic, direct and referral
3. What is broken and what is fixable?
4. Are they investing in paid advertising? Does it seem as if their marketing budget is effective?

In the end the idea is to figure out what works for your competitors and then determine how you can use this information to establish a strong social media strategy. Once you have done this....

Step 3: Humanising the Brand

Most social channels lack a clear sense of personality. Personality in social media is a great opportunity to differentiate your business and become known as standing *for* or *against* something. Whether you sell nails, washing machine spares, tax preparation or dog food, your customers are human beings, and *people* buy from *people*. The blander your industry, the greater the opportunity you have to win by injecting some personality into it. Imagine being the first business in your market with a clearly defined personality and position. Well the chances are that this spot is still up for grabs. Many large brands use social purely as a positioning tool because if they have a large footprint across many countries, it's not always feasible to construct a direct sales approach that works in every territory.

So social media is a fantastic positioning tool to show the world *where* you stand and *what* you stand for. You can then use this positioning to attract more of the customers you *do* want, and put off the sort of customers you *don't want*. Just as every business should have an ideal customer profile, they also have a group that *wouldn't* make good customers.

Luxury brands seek to discourage price shoppers using expensive-looking window displays and elitist social media pictures, while low cost airlines use bold bright logos and advertising to discourage luxury customers who would complain at the lack of (quality) food, the abundance of screaming children and vomit, and the boarding 'experience'. Social media allows you to clearly mark who you *are* and *aren't* suitable for.

Differentiating oneself can seem like a luxury that new businesses can't really afford. I hear from a lot of companies that say "we just need customers, so we're not yet at a stage where we'd want to discourage anyone". What they don't get is that by trying to appeal to everyone, they risk coming across bland. If you have a drug that instantly cures cancer, you can afford to be bland. But if you're selling anything that people can buy from somewhere else online, being bland isn't going to cut it.

Particularly in e-commerce where many stores are selling the same products at around the same price as their competitors, you absolutely have to figure out a way to stand out.

People buy on price when all else is equal. With clever social media positioning you can show that all else *isn't* equal. Whether your business has a strong environmental or ethical ethos (Meridian Food is a great example) or you're particularly customer service orientated (Zappos), these are things that might not be easy to convey during a transaction or a brief introduction. It's only over time and through conscious decisions about how and what to say over social media that you can build these values into your audience's awareness.

We work with around 1,000 small and medium-sized businesses each year through our consultancy and our marketing services. The most noticeable trait of those that struggle is that they have no idea where they fit in their market and what makes them the best choice for customers. If you can't clearly explain why a potential customer should buy from you, chances are that they won't be able to either. It's not enough to build a shop, set some prices and sit and wait. Unless there's a clear reason to buy, people won't. In cases like this, a new website, big ad campaign or aggressive SEO won't make a huge difference. Until the business owner has these answers clear in their own minds, the car has the handbrake on.

The good news is that if this sounds a little *too* familiar to your business, you're sitting on a huge amount of untapped potential. Once you give your customers a compelling reason to buy from you, the handbrake goes off and your marketing becomes a lot more rewarding.

A great example of a small business that uses social media to position and differentiate themselves is wedding photographer Kate Pease (https://www.facebook.com/KatePeasePhotography). Most wedding photographers' posts are pretty dry: "Here are some shots I took of Jane & Peter's wedding last week". To stand out from the noise, in addition to the shots of her brides and grooms, Kate shares tips about how to look good in pictures, and tells the stories behind her weddings. Her personality comes through so strongly in the posts compared to her competitors, and the engagement she gets from her 2,700+ fans shows that her angle appeals.

US advertising photographer Tim Tadder (https://www.facebook.com/TimTadderPhotography) is another example of a photographer using social media well to build his following. His posts combine portfolio work with personality, whilst subtly demonstrating his expertise and authority.

Positioning is especially important for the maker of air conditioning fans, the medical device manufacturer or the plumbers' merchant who is thinking "well this is all OK for companies selling 'cool' consumer-focused products, but what about me?"

The good news is that whatever you sell, your customers are still human beings. If your market is the most boring, commoditised and dull market in the world, you're not going to be the only person thinking this. Your buyers still use social media, and they still have the basic urge to be entertained and happy. Perhaps they don't use social for business, but some will still be on Twitter, Facebook, Instagram or Pinterest in their spare time and while the boss isn't looking at work. If you can be the first company to inject some personality into your market and give your audience something that will actually interest them, then you'll be the one-eyed king in the land of the blind.

Even if there are absolutely no distinguishing features of your product or service and you truly are selling a commodity, you can still inject some personality to build familiarity where none previously existed. The

54

fact that your business *has* a personality through social can become a differentiator for you. Given the choice between purchasing from two identical companies — one who is essentially unknown and one who has been building familiarity through their social media personality, sharing interesting industry-related content and even some off-topic entertainment, and who answers customer service queries through Twitter and Facebook, who would you choose? The social business always wins *when all else is equal.*

The important takeaway is that your business should strive to act like a person and not an entity. So how will you accomplish that?

As a business you need to figure out your brand persona (if your brand was a person what would they be like), tone (what is the vibe of your brand), language (what kind of words will you use when posting on social) and purpose (why you are on social media in the first place.) Purpose was addressed in step one, however brand persona, language and tone can be just as important! Many times you will hear people tell you that business must find their tone and their voice on social - well the voice is the overall defining sound of your businesses personality while the tone refers to the specific execution of that voice. To find your voice, simply find adjectives that best describe your business and/or brand!

Sounds easy right? Marketing Land[2] believes that to truly find your brand's voice, you need to explore the three Cs: culture, community and conversation.

- Culture: what makes your business unique? What makes you stand out? What do you talk about? Let these elements inspire your online voice
- Community: listen to your community and ask them questions so that you can develop the right type of voice that would resonate with the audience you have already established
- Conversation: why are you bringing to the social media table once you've entered the scene?

It might be hard to find the right type of adjectives that describe your business so let's look at an exercise that could help you out:

Exercise - Finding your Voice

In this exercise, we're going to walk through the process of creating your voice and ultimately your tone. A great place to start is asking questions. Such as:

- Why did you start your company?

---

[2] http://marketingland.com/20-great-social-media-voices-and-how-to-develop-your-own-18057

- If your brand were a person, what kind of personality would it have?
- How does your brand make you feel and how do you want it make other people feel?
- If your brand was a person, what's their relationship to the consumer?
- What other brand voices do you admire?
- Describe in adjectives what your company's personality is not.
- Are there any companies that have a similar personality to yours? Why are they similar?
- What are three words that best describe your company?

It might be hard at first but every brand has a defining tone and voice that helps them interact with their target audience. Nike's tagline "Just Do It' provides an inspirational voice for people on and off the field, while toilet paper company Charmin decided to use a humourous and light-hearted voice with their popular hashtag #Tweetfromtheseat.

Charmin @Charmin · Nov 7

Happy #BookLoversDay What is your go-to book on the throne? #TweetFromTheSeat

Still can't figure out your voice and/or the adjectives that might describe your company? Then ask around! Ask friends, family and customers about how they see your company and you might find it's more obvious to those outside the business than those on the inside!

Next we need to translate that voice into a tone. Depending on what social media channel you choose to use, the tone can be different depending on the channel and on the type of interaction that you may have - from a happy customer to a frustrated one. As a result, it is probably best to work from a template. We personally like the one provided by Rocket Media that recommends first coming up with content types that require a certain tone then filling in the details in a template like this:

58

Content type: What are you writing?
Reader: Who are you talking to in this scenario?
Reader feelings: What's the reader feeling when they are in this tone scenario?
Your tone should be: Use adjectives that describe how you should sound in this scenario.
Write like this: Give a brief example of how the writing should sound.
Tips: Explain best practices of writing for this scenario.

...an example of a filled out template could look like:

Content Type: Tweets
Reader: Customers, fans and potential customers
Reader feelings: captivated and intrigued to learn more
Your tone should be: informative, approachable, jovial and clear
Write like this: "I've lived in & traveled in #latinamerica. So the question is, should you go? http://buff.ly/1NXPcxy #ttot #travel"
Tips: avoid industry jargon, try not to be too colloquial, avoid excessive use of exclamation points, and be clear and direct. Don't avoid negative comments but address them head on!

If this is a little too intense for you than you can simplify the process by simply asking 4 questions: What is your voice? How should you write? How shouldn't you write? Why?

Once you find your perfect voice and how you will be projecting that voice through your tone, make sure that you always remember that on social media the most important thing when you communicate on all channels is that your brand and/or business is 1) authentic and 2) consistent. People don't want to talk to companies, they want to talk to human beings and they want to be able to rely on them.

Step 4: Create a Channel Plan

So you've created your customer persona, researched your competitors, created your voice/tone and learned the dos and don'ts of being on social. Now you're ready to start working on specific channels. **But wait: which channels will you be most active on?**

Facebook has over a billion monthly active users; Twitter has over 300 million monthly active users with a billion unique visits monthly to sites with embedded Tweets; Instagram has a community of 400 million members with an average of 80 million photos shared per day. In reality, there is a lot of noise out there. Businesses, especially small businesses, need to be strategic when they choose what social media channels they would like to have a presence on.

In the end you can't be on everything especially if you have a limited amount of time, budget and manpower.

It is a common misconception that curated content does not need to be adapted for different channels but can be blasted into the social media ethos. However, this is not the best idea as each channel as a very distinct type of user and social media strategies need to be adapted depending on where you want to be most active. Instagram, according to the Iconosquare Instagram 2015 study, is ideal for brands and businesses that focus on fashion, decoration and culture and not the best channel for businesses that focus on real-estate, health and/or finance. Furthermore, Instagram is perfect for businesses that target individuals between the ages of 15 - 35 as 73% of Instagram users are within that age bracket. So if you are business focusing on, for example, geriatrics, then Instagram probably isn't the best avenue for you.

Now that you already have created your ideal customer and done some research about your current customer and (maybe) fan base, you should have a good idea of their demographics, attitudes and emotions — basically you should know your ideal customer inside out. So where do they spend the most time? Are they DIY obsessed? Maybe Pinterest is the way to go. Do they have a lot of question and need on-going support? Then maybe Facebook or Twitter would work. Most likely your goals will be different on each social platform, which means that the content you develop and share needs to be different as well. Here are some great components that you need to take in consideration provided by Joe Pulizzi, founder of the Content Marketing Institute, in the Social Media Examiner:

- Which Channel? (Facebook? Twitter?)
- The Customer Persona (who will you be targeting?)
- The Goal (Is it a sales goal, cost-savings goal or are you trying to create a better customer experience?)
- Primary Content Type (Textual, video, infographics?)
- Structure (What does a general post look like?)
- Tone (Playful, sarcastic?)
- Channel Integration (How will this channel work with your other channels for maximum impact?)
- Desired Action (What user behavior do you want to achieve?)
- Editorial Plan (Every channel needs its own editorial calendar.)

After you nailed down specifics, it's time to start setting up your accounts and posting engaging, authentic and consistent content on all the social media channels that you've deemed appropriate.

Step 5: Analyse and Adapt

So you've created your accounts and have been posting on social media for a couple of weeks now and three things might be happening: your presence on social is growing, it hasn't moved or it's not resonating with your customers. It is time to do a social audit!

Analytics are your friends, the most important one will be Google Analytics followed closely by the analytics provided by the various social media channels that you are using, such as Facebook Analytics and/or Twitter Analytics. If you have a bigger budget, then we would recommend signing up for a special tool that focuses primarily on social audits like TrueSocialMetrics and/or PageKarma. These types of programs are designed specifically for marketers and are deeply rooted in the day-to-day practice of leading brands' social profiles management. They also at times have pretty cool features, for example PageKarma allows you to not only compare your social media page and its numbers with your competitors but it has other cool features like letting you analyse the Ambassadors of any Facebook page to help understand and improve your targeting strategy.

If you do not have the budget for these third-party programs, then focus all your energy on the free analytics tools provided by each social media channel. Pull the data from the last month and look at what did well, what didn't do well, who interacted the most? Was it females or males? How old were they? All this information can then be compared with your customer persona and adaptations can be made either to your persona or to your social media strategy. Social is not about creating a strategy and then just letting it go — it is constantly evolving and businesses need to constantly analyzing and adapting their strategies to keep up with the evolving social media world!

The Three Ms of a Successful Social Media Campaign

So what makes the difference between a campaign that goes *good* viral, one that goes *bad* viral and one that goes absolutely nowhere?

The secret is to think of your social media marketing just like any other form of marketing. Where things go wrong is when people expect that social media — just because it's social, and it's cool and trendy — is going to do the work for them. This inevitably ends in disappointment. The basic principles of marketing have to be obeyed in every channel, and at Exposure Ninja we define these basic principles as the three Ms:

1. Finding and creating the right **m**essage
2. Targeting the right **m**arket
3. Using the right **m**ethods of communication (advertising media)

These three principles are the difference between a social media campaign that goes viral, engages people and brings new traffic to your business, and one that disappears without a trace.

Let's look at the construction of a great campaign, starting with *message.*

Finding Your Right Message

The message and tone that you use across your social campaigns is a key predictor of how successful they will be. As we've seen in the examples previously, a good message will resonate with your target audience and engage them. A lifeless or unclear message will fall through the cracks.

By identifying your goal in the previous step, you're already part way there. For most businesses, it's just too tempting to head straight to Facebook and start creating a business page, or go to Twitter and start Tweeting. But setting off without a map makes it unlikely that the journey will end somewhere rewarding.

Businesses who have a clear online message tend to receive more followers. A definite personality behind the brand, even if it's not tied to a particular person, helps make it seem more human. That's the entire goal of a social media campaign: give your business a human personality that people identify and want to be friends (or at least want to associate) with.

Clear messages are easiest to see at the extremities: really cheap companies who adopt a confrontational 'us against the world in our crusade for low prices' stance, versus luxury brands that take an 'only the finest will do' stance. Each of these has its place and will appeal to a certain type of customer.

Low budget customers who perceive the world as a grand conspiracy to rip them off and exploit them will identify with a budget airline crusading against anyone trying to increase charges against their customers, whether it's a government increasing fuel duty or an entire country increasing air taxes.

Meanwhile high-end customers might appreciate the smug confidence of Gucci's profile, which doesn't talk about anything other than the brand and how fantastic their products are. Almost 800,000 Twitter followers don't seem to mind reading about this every day because that's what they *expect* from Gucci. It's a message that is consistent with the brand. What they understand is that their fans want to buy into and experience a taste of the Gucci world. The value to their audience comes from association with Gucci as opposed to Gucci's sharing of relevant and useful information. Gucci wouldn't mock their competitors or Tweet cat jokes, yet for some businesses this sort of strategy would be far more effectively than constantly talking about their own products.

Your social media message doesn't have to be as extreme as this, but elements from examples like these can be adopted and adapted to suit your audience.

Overall, it is important that you decide your angle in advance and try to stick to it.

Often a brand's social personality follows that of the business owner. Think Virgin for example. Richard Branson's easygoing style and healthy disrespect for established practices (and businesses) come through loud and clear in most Virgin social channels.

Targeting The Right Market

So you've got a goal for your social campaign, and you might be starting to have ideas about the sort of message and personality that you want to convey. Next up is identifying the right audience. This is simpler in some markets than others. My brother makes electrical connectors for oilrig drills. His target audience is pretty clear — people that are building or maintaining a certain type of oil rig. Meanwhile my sister makes sportswear and jackets. Her company's target market could be pretty much anyone aged 18-40, and unless we narrow that audience significantly (or divide it into smaller niches), advertising costs will be high, engagement will be low and there will be a lot of wastage because we can't tap into the specific passions and use a laser targeted message.

While you might have a few different types of target customer it's likely that they will all have something in common. After all it's probably this that draws them to you in the first place. Perhaps it's their appreciation of being treated like an individual, their taste for quality, or their love of a bargain. This should become the basis of your core message.

Niche Customer Targeting

For some businesses, their target customer fits into a relatively narrow profile. Their message can be a laser, precisely focused on this group. Marketing to a niche is usually preferable, so it's sometimes important to split a larger audience into smaller niches.

If I'm a personal trainer selling my service to fitness enthusiasts readying themselves for a physique competition, all of my social content will be stuff that people new to fitness wouldn't necessarily understand or identify with. Whereas if I'm mostly helping people lose weight after a life of inactivity, I can target my message around topics like getting active and tips to stay moving at the workplace. Each of these messages is really relevant to one audience but almost meaningless to the other, despite the fact that they're both coming from a personal trainer.

The challenge of how to serve two markets simultaneously is often a distraction from the reality that most businesses in this situation should jump two feet into the one market they are best at serving, and exclude the other.

If we take a look at three examples of businesses that play in the sportswear retail market we can see how each has identified a particular type of customer at the exclusion of others, and how this has allowed them to grow in their particular niche. JD Sports, Sports Direct and Sweaty Betty all sell clothing and accessories for sports, yet their target audiences are quite different. At the time of writing, all three are advertising 'SALE' using their Twitter cover photos, but how they present the sale in their content is interesting. Their social media communications are so in tune with their core brand messages, that most people familiar with the three companies would have no trouble identifying messages from any of them. Generic social media this is not.

JD Sports (@JDSportsFashion) understands that their audience is not bargain basement, price-driven customers but those who want the latest, newest and trendiest sportswear. Their feed reflects this as they share new products, background information and pictures. As their Twitter handle suggests, a large portion of their market isn't particularly driven by sports *performance* but rather sports *fashion*. This approach works well when sales are the goal, but their social feed is never particularly 'salesy'. They avoid publishing 'buy' links or strong calls to action, for example, trusting that their customers know where to go if they want the products that they see. The purpose of the Twitter account then is to collect an audience who is passionate about the latest in sportswear fashion and associate the JD Sports brand with this.

Sports Direct meanwhile caters to a much wider market united by one common thread: price. They use a permanent 'All stock must go' heavily discounted angle to attract a wide variety of price-driven customers, whether or not these customers are into sport. This means their customer profile is too wide to make any specific product-driven strategy effective, so instead they take a more general approach focusing on sporting events, weather and cheering for UK athletes. Because of the variation in their audience interests, they can't really even focus too heavily on individual sports for fear of alienating large parts of their audience that aren't into that sport. The result is more of a standard awareness campaign intended to boost the visibility of Sports Direct in their customers' daily lives, whilst also giving the brand a personality that price-driven retailers can often lack.

Sweaty Betty's target audience is much narrower; specifically affluent women who are into fitness. Their customers aren't price driven and are more interested in looking good and the feeling of exclusivity from buying a higher-end brand. Because their audience is so narrow, they are able to focus on specific product-promotion, information on certain fitness trends and promotion of articles mentioning Sweaty Betty. It's an example of a positioning and alignment approach ("we are all women into fitness just like you") whilst they also seek to add value with content likely to be of interest to their audience.

So here we see three companies all selling sports clothing, targeting very different audiences, but using their social media profiles to grow their herd. For many businesses, the difference between profitable and unprofitable social media is understanding their audience and crafting a message engaging enough to keep them interested long enough to influence a purchase. In that sense, companies with a narrow audience like Sweaty Betty and JD Sports are at an advantage, because audience targeting is easier for them than for a price or convenience-driven business with a wider audience.

Wide Customer Targeting

An example of a business whose target customer is spread across numerous demographics, interests and geographic areas is Nespresso. Having a coffee is an everyday habit but Nespresso markets it as an extraordinary experience. The design, the quality of coffee in each cup and the varieties are what (they hope) makes drinking a Nespresso coffee a magical and emotionally awakening occurrence. Their tagline is simple: *What Else?* As if there are no other options out there is as great as a nice hot cup of Nespresso espresso.

To the untrained eye, their targeting might seem wide. However through research, listening, competitor comparisons and social media audits, brands like Nespresso can pinpoint the types of people that are buying their products and map out their details in order to craft a specific customer persona. So let's take a look at Nespresso's Twitter page and try to figure out whom they are trying to target.

First off we notice that Nespresso is a luxury brand so even though it sells coffee it is not in direct competition with brands like Starbucks or Kenco. Luxury means that Nespresso focuses on people with jobs and pay scales. The second question is what these types of people enjoy doing during their free time. Scrolling down the Nespresso Global Twitter page some customer profiles jump out: foodie, art lover, luxury traveler, and golfer. There are also some indications of welfare and environmental-mindedness through the sprinkling of posts about their sustainability and development work, which creates trust and dependability.

Nespresso Global @Nespresso · Oct 31
Would you pair butternut squash with coffee? Try this surprising
#halloween recipe: bit.ly/1KMlJzd

↩   ⇅ 3   ≣   ♥ 5   •••

No matter what type of individual they are targeting, whether it is the luxury traveler or foodie, Nespresso tie their content to their coffee. For example, the food recipes made by world famous chefs usually have coffee in them. They also have a very distinct and consistent voice and strategy. Their photos are often overhead pictures of a cup of Nespresso on a table with some desirable object beside the cup whether it is a camera, or a travel magazine — they always tie their product into it. In the end, what's better than to dream about far away lands while sipping a cup of Nespresso? Their image and message is well crafted and their audience, although it seems wide, is extremely specific. Nespresso's social page doesn't sell a product, it sells an experience. To further solidify this experience, Nespresso has created a luxury hashtag #AtelierNespresso and emotional hashtags like #nespressomoments and #nespressopassions. An excellent example is a Tweet showcasing a cup of coffee, a pair of reader's glasses, a summer hat and a book with the caption: Summer reading, coffee dreaming #NespressoPassions

And to make sure that all their geographically important regions are touched upon, Nespresso has created multiple Twitter and Facebook pages for specific regions tied together by a global page.

What to do if your target audience doesn't use social media

Some businesses will assume that their core audience doesn't use social media. Even if this is true (which it often isn't. Even people in the most boring industries use *some* social media, if not for work) it doesn't necessarily mean that it can't be a profitable use of time and energy.

As well as the SEO benefits (which we discuss in another chapter), there are networking opportunities open to businesses wanting to establish new profitable relationships with others in their industry.

One of our clients is a luxury home technology company whose customers are often wealthy foreign businessmen with homes in the UK. This sort of customer isn't going to be Tweeting them questions about home automation wiring any time soon. In fact, most of their customers aren't involved in the buying decisions at all. But by providing an up-to-date and aspirational social media profile covering the latest in home technology and interiors, they can attract an audience of interior design companies and other businesses involved in high end home renovation. Following, Retweeting and interacting with these potential business partners and sources of referrals means they can be actively involved in building an online community around this market.

So if your reaction is that your audience doesn't use social media, firstly check that assumption and secondly find an audience for that *does* and can still make you money from.

Fine Tuning Your Message Over Time

It's important not to stress about getting your message 100% right first time. You might find that your audience doesn't behave exactly the way you expected, and therefore you need to slightly adjust what you say to them. You might find that your audience varies by social network as well. Over time you'll learn what sort of content really appeals to your fans and how you can structure any promotions to maximise engagement.

We've got clients that have been in 'deciding mode' on social media for *two years*. They started umming and ahhing about it so long ago, that any plans they put together are already out of date. Rather than spending too long worrying and asking the 'What if?' questions, the important thing is just to *start*. If you're active and willing to experiment, you will find an approach that works for you and gives you the results that you're after, even if it takes a little time. Accept that it's not going to be perfect right off the bat, keep your eyes open and be receptive to feedback about how well your campaign is being received.

Choosing Your Method

So far we have thought about our **M**essage, which is designed to appeal to our audience and celebrate what makes us different. We then sought to understand our **M**arket, helping us to hone and focus this message to have the biggest impact amongst our audience.

The third step is choosing your **M**ethod of communication. We'll be looking at getting to grips with each of the social channels in the next section of the book, but for now it's important to start thinking about where your audience is most likely to spend time online so you can meet them where they already hang out. As we'll see, each audience has it's preferred networks and what might work well for a brand on Twitter could do nothing for the same brand if applied to Pinterest for example.

Figures from the Pew Research Centre's Demographics of Key Social Networking Platforms gives us some interesting stats on relative social media popularity and demographic. Facebook is the network used by the largest total number of Internet users (71% of US adult internet users), with Twitter, Pinterest and Instagram at 23%, 28% and 26% respectively. Twitter is slightly more popular amongst men, but image-based Instagram and Pinterest are more popular with women — particularly Pinterest, which women are more than three times more likely to use than men. The research also shows that as household income rises, so does Pinterest use, matching the experience of many in the Internet marketing world who have seen high-end female-oriented products sell particularly well as a result of Pinterest sharing. Instagram has also seen an increase in popularity amongst higher income families, making its advertising platform even more interesting.

Remember to claim your free online marketing review, if you haven't done so already, at www.exposureninja.com/review one of our expert social media team will send you free personal recommendations, competitor analysis and suggestions to grow your audience.

Viral Growth Secrets of the Pros

In this section we'll be looking at some Ninja strategies that you can use to grow your following and boost your profile. But before we dive in, it's worth talking more about goals. A significant percentage of the readers of this book are looking to increase the number of likes, follows and other metrics that indicate popularity, and that's basically it. While it's clearly a worthy goal to expand your audience, we encourage people to think in terms of increasing their follower quality and relevance as well. Your goal for your social media campaign should not be purely quantity-driven ("I want to have 3,000 followers by June"), but rather driven by what we call *profitable influence*. Profitable influence is different to regular influence because - surprise surprise - it focuses on getting attention likely to turn into money.

Rather than aim purely for volume then, a profitable social media campaign will raise your profile *amongst people who can give you money or have access to others who can give you money*. Everything else is just a pleasant but unnecessary ego boost. The ideal result is that when buyers of your product or service are in the moment of need, you are there at the front of their mind. This doesn't happen overnight and it takes time.

Let's look at a real world example of *profitable influence* in action:

You're looking to book your family into a dentist in your area for a check up. You Google "dentists" and open a few tabs. One of the dentists mentions that new patients who 'like' their Facebook page get free teeth whitening. There's a button to 'like' the page right underneath the offer, with a call to action that says "Like us Now for your Free Teeth Whitening", so you click it. While you're clicking around the other dentists in your area, you find another one that you like the look of because they're slightly closer.

You book in and pay this competitor a visit, but you're not overly impressed. They tried to sell you expensive treatments you didn't think you needed and the office was tatty. You decide that you're unlikely to go back, but for the time being your itch was scratched and you won't need to find a new dentist until your next checkup is due.

Meanwhile, your Facebook 'like' on the first dentist's page still stands. Luckily for them, they've read lots of great social media books and they're providing lots of genuinely useful content on their page that appeals to potential customers, not just those who need a dentist right now. This social savvy dentist posts blogs on their website about things like "The most common tooth brushing mistake - are you inadvertently damaging your teeth twice per day?" "Is tooth whitening dangerous? How to get white teeth without causing long-term damage", "How to teach your kids how to brush their teeth" and "How to choose the best toothbrush (TIP: the most expensive ones are NOT the best!)". These are all things that ordinary people would find interesting and actually useful.

This dentist doesn't go crazy promoting blog posts three times a day, because people just don't *need* that much tooth information in their lives. But over the course of a year let's say we see fifteen articles of real interest posted by this dentist and we click on and read five of these. That means we've been to their site five times and are familiar with them, their personality, and the dental practice. This puts them miles ahead of the other dentists in our town, who remain completely anonymous.

When it comes time to book that next check up, one of two things will happen:

1. We enquire with the Facebook dentist first, as we're already familiar and have built a small amount of rapport with them.
2. We'll search "dentist" again, ask a friend for a recommendation, or embark on any other dentist-finding operation. During the course of this research phase, we're drawn to mentions of the Facebook dentist. We recognise their name, we feel safe with them and we remember that we've got that free tooth whitening treatment with our first appointment.

Either way, that dentist's social media activity has just greatly increased their chances of making a sale. If they can deliver a great experience, then this social campaign is also going to boost repeat business as they stick in our minds and continue to build rapport between appointments as well.

Over a number of years, that dentist becomes a real part of our consciousness and gets access to our attention *infinitely more* than her competitors, who are invisible in our day-to-day life. This dentist doesn't have to be better, cheaper or more convenient - those things are totally irrelevant. Their competitive advantage is *familiarity and rapport*. And in a world where few businesses have any competitive advantage at all, that's enough!

In this way, social media allows you to boost your profile amongst your target audience no matter how high profile you are by other metrics. If you scan through your own Facebook timeline, Twitter or Instagram feed you'll notice that there are businesses, seminar speakers and other entities that are really a part of your *daily* or even *hourly* consciousness due to their intelligent use of social media. They're probably not the most famous businesses, speakers and others that you know of, and they might not even be the *best*, but they're the ones you remember and are familiar with.

Viral Growth Strategy 1. Piggybacking Celebrity

Never have we had such easy access to the thought-leaders in our fields. On Twitter they're just an @reply away, and everybody can see their communication in public. We humans seem to have a keen fascination with celebrities, and their opinions hold a lot of weight. But what most people want from celebrities above anything else is *access*; to feel like they're part of the in crowd. As long as people can observe their favourite celebrity - whether that person is a TV personality, fitness guru or business leader - they'll continue to be hooked on social.

It doesn't stop at observation though. With Twitter in particular we can start to build relationships and associations with these celebrities and authorities, which can obviously give our business some juicy exposure. Nothing will replace real solid personal relationships involving handshakes and lunches, but for those of us who are too busy *doing* to be out schmoozing, social can give us a handy shortcut when we want to 'borrow' authority from established figures.

Something as simple as a Retweet can be a significant implied endorsement. It says to the authority's followers: "this person says what I'm thinking so I don't even need to comment". If that authority figure is in your industry or market, a Retweet like this can generate a decent boost in follower numbers and significantly elevate your position in the minds of the clan. Keep reading to find out how to attract this sort of Retweet.

A conversation with an authority figure can do the same. Providing the conversation is natural and equal, it can raise your profile amongst both your followers and the followers of the authority.

Getting High Profile Retweets and Starting Conversations

So how do you go about getting Retweeted or starting a conversation with an authority figure in your industry?

The first step is to find someone that has a history of responding and Retweeting. Some authorities/celebrities treat Twitter purely as a broadcast medium and follow very few people.

Just like anybody else, the question running through his or her heads the whole time is *"What's in it for me?"* There has to be a clear benefit to them if they are going to share your post or reply to you. On social media, this clear benefit is usually a feeling of *significance*. Anything they RT or reply to is usually something that strengthens their position of authority or reinforces a principle or idea that they are known for promoting; it could be recognition of their impact; it could be a piece of news that would give them significance for promoting to their followers.

Imagine that your target celebrity has just released a new book. They want *so badly* to constantly tell their audience how proud they are of this new book and tell them to go out and buy it now. But this wouldn't look classy, so they bite their lip and stay schtum about the book. You come along and Tweet them something along the lines of "Loving @celebrity's new book! Great ideas for customer service in chapter 3!" This is *exactly* what they wanted to say but could never say themselves, so your chances of being Retweeted go up exponentially. Remember to make the Tweet short enough so that they can share it with your @twitter handle, and also make a comment and still get it under the 140-character limit.

We'll look at timing your Tweets in more detail in the Twitter section, but for now one of the keys to getting your target celebrity to actually see your message is Tweeting them at a time of day when they are most active. If they're getting sixty replies per hour and you Tweet them three hours before they check their feed, your chance of being seen 180th in their feed is small. To find out the optimal time to Tweet your celebrity, look back through their history to see patterns of activity and notice when they tend to be most responsive. Are they flicking through Twitter just after they wake up, at lunch and while they're on the toilet? Probably yes, yes and yes! Keep in mind that they could be using automatic post scheduling software (which we'll look at in the Tools section), in which case try to analyse the times of day that they are having conversations with followers rather than just Tweeting.

But remember one of the things that you want to avoid is Tweeting the celebrity with a Tweet that adds absolutely no value. For example: H*ey @celebrity you like cars? Check out my website!* Just because they have expressed interest in something doesn't mean that they want to be spammed, and your chance of a response is low.

Finding a new audience

If your business has traditionally been selling to one type of customer and you want to transition to a new demographic or add different niches to your customer market, social is a great platform to do that. Identifying a leading figure in a new market and piggybacking their authority can be extremely profitable, and it's something we've used with great effect.

Running contests and promoting content to bloggers in a particular scene can help you pick up interest from their followers and give you a head start in a new market. In a campaign that we ran for an LED lighting e-commerce client, one of our Social/PR Ninjas with her own popular blog created a Halloween DIY project using one of their products. By writing a detailed instructional for the project, she exposed this product to an entirely new audience who perhaps wouldn't previously have considered buying LED lights.

Men's footwear company Oliver Sweeney used social media to promote a new driving shoe by tapping into car manufacturer Jaguar's audience. Oliver Sweeney's own posts usually receive 100-200 likes on Instagram. But when Jaguar posted a picture of the shoe on their Instagram page, it received over 13,000 likes in less than an hour. Oliver Sweeney identified that Jaguar had a large and relevant audience, and the collaboration significantly increased the exposure of their brand to this audience. If they offered Jaguar 100% of the profit from the shoe, that still would have been a great deal for the access to Jaguar's following that they received. This type of 'celebrity' endorsement (and 'celebrity' is used to mean anyone with a following) is the quickest way to build credibility and launch you into a new arena.

Who does your audience admire, and how could you piggyback on their profile? What could you do for them, and how could you make this a win for them too? Is there an incentive you could offer them so that they want you to succeed? Small scale influencers might be persuaded if you ask nicely, but usually the ones you really want will need some skin in the game. Whether it's affiliate or joint venture commission, free product or reciprocal promotion, we'll look at how to do effective outreach later on.

Authority outreach

Each time you write a blog post (and we'll look later at how to write genuinely useful and important blog posts), think about which authorities in your market might be interested in this topic.

If you're a hair salon looking to increase your visibility online with celebrity haircut deconstructions, Tweeting each celebrity's fan club page can bag you some easy visibility when they share your tutorial with thousands of people who want to look like that celebrity. An automotive e-commerce site can create a post around building a replica of a famous rally car, and Tweet it to the driver. If they Retweet it, that's targeted and relevant visibility in front of a ton of car fans.

At Exposure Ninja we also use social media to find authority bloggers to work with on running giveaways and promotions. On Twitter, using hashtags like #freebiefriday #win #bloggerswanted and #mummybloggers can attract interest from bloggers looking for giveaway prizes or products to review. If you can give them something relevant that works with their audience, and you can provide them with an angle to write a blog post about, you can get some significant visibility on their blogs. We outreached to blogger IAlwaysBelievedInFutures in this way, and ended up running a contest and blog post that attracted 844 entrants for a contest and promoted our client, an e-commerce site selling the prize those entrants had just expressed desire for. We've given away hotel stays, home products, adventure days… in fact, if you've got a blog make sure you follow @exposureninjapr and see what sort of goodies you might be able to pick up!

Creating Viral Content

Creating particularly share worthy content requires some thought and, yes, a little hard work. Spur of the moment offers ("10% off" - boring!) or updates about your business ("new website!" - who cares?) just aren't going to stand out from the 4.5 Billion other pages on the Internet.

Here are some content creation strategies to boost your social sharing and raise your authority. Some are easy, some require more effort; some are cheap, some involve an investment. Rather than head straight for the easy ones (that's what everyone else will do), seriously consider the ones that make you uncomfortable or stretch you outside your comfort zone:

- Industry surveys are a relatively easy way to make a big splash in your market, attract a bunch of links (good for SEO) and grow your social following at the same time. This doesn't have to be any more complicated than setting up a questionnaire in Google Drive (free) and surveying your audience, customers or industry peers. If your questions are geared towards generating insights that aren't commonly known, or you are able to quantify a pattern or trend that you see developing, the results of this survey could be very interesting to your market. The best way to use survey results for viral growth is to first publish them on your website or blog, then link to it from your social media updates. That way, any shares or links the survey gets are directed at your website (again, good for SEO), and whilst people are on your site you have the opportunity to convert them to leads. Don't forget also to collect the details of respondents so that you can notify everyone who participated once the results are published. Invite them to share the results on their own social feeds and you'll pick up yet more visibility. If your survey results are significant enough publications and news outlets might take interest, write up a few key takeaways into a short piece and send it over to journalists and editors who talk on your topic - you'd be amazed at how easy it is to get some press coverage with a good survey. The headline of your pitch is key, and key stats can make a popular choice for an attention grabbing statement. For tips on journalist outreach, see the SEO/PR section in our bestselling book How To Get To The Top Of Google.

- Review products or services that are relevant to your audience. Give plenty of details and include rich media (pictures, videos, embedded Tweets) to make the review as valuable and comprehensive as possible, and increase time on page. You can include 'Tweetables' - key facts and insights that your readers might want to Tweet - and use a service like www.clicktoTweet.com to enable your readers to Tweet these with a couple of clicks. Remember to include your own twitter handle and your blog link in the Tweetable, so that any Tweets your audience send out promote both you and your website. Again if you can find a headline in there ("Has X Just Rendered All Other Ys Obsolete?" or "X Stuns the ABC Industry with a revolutionary take on Z") then you are more likely to attract the attention of the people you need. Remember that if you're writing positive reviews, the business providing the product or service might be interested to see the review once it's live, and might Retweet a link to the review that you @reply them in.
- Give future predictions, particularly if you can remark on something close to the hearts of others in your industry, again thinking about an eye catching headline: "The Game Changer for Small Businesses: How small business online

marketing just changed forever and what you need to do immediately to survive". I defy any small business owner's interest NOT to be peaked there... Vogue's 'Six New Season Style Rules' is good, as is '6 Interior Design Trends To Watch For In 2016'.

- Interview leading figures about the future of your industry. Publish the interview on your website, then post it out on social media tagging the industry figure involved. If they're like most people, they'll then Retweet this as it boosts their credibility in the eyes of their audience. As always include a catchy or controversial headline, and plenty of Tweetable quotes using www.clicktoTweet.com.

The Ninja Rules of Success for Social Media Content are:

1. Publish it on your website first. If it generates a lot of shares, you want to make sure these links are pointing at *your* site rather than anyone else's. The only exception is when you are writing for a high-profile publication for credibility. Even then, you might decide to write a background piece on your own blog and link to your piece on the authority site.

2. Good headlines generate clicks. "7 Ways to..." "Five quick tips for successful..." "The shocking truth about..." "You won't believe what happened when..." If you're thinking that this all

93

sounds a bit sensationalist and 'Buzzfeed-y' then... you're right! But it works. Of course you and I are much too sophisticated to fall prey to such obvious headlines as these, right? Any serious marketing student can do worse than study the headlines on the trashiest tabloid newspaper websites. Anyone that can generate 133 comments in 3 hours for an article about a TV show host saying the word "Cult" has my respect (See Daily Mail article "Wash your mouth out, Ruth! Viewers shocked to hear This Morning presenter insult Eamonn Holmes with a VERY rude word... but did they mishear?" http://www.dailymail.co.uk/news/article-3317166/Wash-mouth-Ruth-Viewers-shocked-hear-Morning-presenter-insult-Eamonn-Holmes-rude-word-did-mishear.html Clue: yes, they misheard)

3. Include a brief summary at the start of a longer piece so people interested can bookmark it for later, or share without reading the whole thing. Remember that people use social media to fill spare *minutes* not hours, so making it easy to digest your content is important. This isn't to say it should lack substance, but you should aim to give people with only a couple of spare minutes enough value to make them want to return later. You'll notice the most viral sites tend to keep articles fairly short and encourage grazing behaviour with links to other related

articles, constantly trying to draw the reader to the next piece before they get decide to leave the site. The longer you can keep people and the more engaged they are, the better visibility your site will get both on Google and Facebook, which we believe both use usage metrics to influence ranking.

4. Make sure your website works well on mobile. According to our own research from over 400 websites that we manage, traffic from social media tends to be between 65-80% mobile users, depending on the market. According to the Pew Research Centre, every single online news outlet now receives the majority of their traffic from mobile, with the percentage varying between 60% (Daily Mail) and 80% (Buzzfeed). If your site isn't mobile friendly then you're losing sales and visitors every single day through lower visibility and higher bounce rate. What's more, it's not enough for your site to just 'technically' be mobile friendly. It actually needs to be easy to use and give as good an experience as it does on desktop.

5. If you can tie in a current event or celebrity, people's radars will already be tuned to receive your message. As a fairly recent example, take a look at the number of hair transplant articles that mention English footballer Wayne Rooney to see how you can piggyback on celebrity news for maximum exposure. Most of the

clinics using him in their stories had no affiliation to him whatsoever, but recognised that even just mentioning him implied endorsement and made it more likely their content would be shared. Now it had general interest.

Using Controversy

Controversy is a great way to become active and engaged in your market, particularly if you are offering a new way of doing things, or you want to be perceived as such.

If you know that your customers have a gripe or distaste for how things are usually done in your industry, siding with them to stand against the established players can build affinity and trust.

As an example, I've come to hate most SEO companies who aren't transparent about the strategies they are using. By continuing to do what they *used to do* to promote websites in 2009, are getting their innocent clients penalised. The good news is that most of the world's businesses *also* hate this lack of transparency. So by arming them with the knowledge and strategies to fight this 'enemy' (rubbish SEO companies), we can show how we're different and position ourselves in a way that makes us stand out.

If we were in a position to need more clients and confrontation was consistent with our values, we could start calling out some of the cowboys over social media. If I am happy to wave my arms around and kick up enough of a fuss, this 'war' will be played out in public and generate publicity for Exposure Ninja. We can write press releases, make videos, do live Q&As about the situation and knock on the door of industry magazines and blogs to generate even more publicity. If the enemy is smart they'll play along because they'll *also* be generating publicity for themselves. With good damage limitation and smart strategy even the 'victim' in these sorts of stunts can quite easily come out of the other side with their reputation unscathed but profile raised.

If you look at Donald Trump's very public 'war' with Rosie O'Donnell for example (which incidentally was timed carefully to coincide with the new series of The Apprentice), both parties benefitted from a profile boost and saw their TV and print exposure increase as a result. Stories about the feud spread over social media and continue to do so every time either of them needs a bit of publicity. While this is a high profile example, the tactic can be useful to businesses of any size that don't mind a little public argy bargy.

In my opinion the ultimate master of courting controversy to boost his own profile and grow his business is @KimDotcom, the founder of Megaupload and its new incarnation Mega. His services are used by Internet users around the world, but his primary and most profitable target audience is those who upload and download pirated software, games and music using his sites. Kim is absolutely magnetic to this market with his unique mixture of part underdog, part pirate, and part obnoxiously rich troublemaker. He's all too happy to speak out publicly against any establishment from the US government to Hollywood rights holders, and a good dose of his outrageous 'you can't catch me' personality makes for extremely entertaining viewing.

Managing to strike this fine balance between power (his Megaupload site was estimated to be responsible for 4% of all internet traffic at its peak) and victimisation (he lives in New Zealand and is constantly fighting extradition attempts), his audience regards him as a demi-god. By posting pictures of his massive house, helicopters, jets — even one of him holding a gun in front of a Mercedes with the numberplate 'Guilty' — each of his new online businesses generates a phenomenal amount of publicity and awareness. It's a brilliant strategy that costs him nothing. Aside from the legal fees for his sites, obviously!

Controversy without ruffling feathers

Some readers will feel uneasy at the idea of courting controversy because they're naturally averse to confrontation. But not all controversy is created equal, and not all of it actually requires confrontation. Much like Orwell's Two Minutes Hate, a lot of apparent controversy can be generated by picking a fight against an enemy that can't or won't fight back, or even that doesn't exist. This strategy can also be summed up as 'finding a parade to stand in front of'.

If we take a look at the outpouring of emotion against SOPA (the Stop Online Piracy Act) that resulted in online protests from thousands of websites and millions of web users, the object of this mammoth focus of public hate was US legislators. It became clear quite early on that online public support was heavily in favour of blocking SOPA, and that the legislators weren't going to launch a meaningful resistance. By choosing an enemy like this to 'campaign' against, many savvy social media users used the STOP SOPA movement to raise their own profile and build authority. They stood in front of an existing parade against an enemy that refused to defend itself.

Every industry has a common enemy in some shape, whether it's the 'old guard', legislation, trends or fashions, snobbery, elitism, vulgarity or ignorance. If you're stuck for ideas, ask yourself 'what would you end up bitching about if you and your ideal customer started drinking together?'

By positioning yourself against this enemy you can tap into the conversation your audience is already having in their heads. If your message resonates with how your audience already thinks about something they feel strongly, you'll get shares, likes and plenty of supportive comments.

Using Hashtags and Existing Conversations

Originating on Twitter, hashtags are a way that an audience can categorise or 'tag' their posts by a certain theme. When people are interested in a certain hashtag - for example if they are following a particular event - they might search for other Tweets using that hashtag to see what people are saying about it. By tagging your posts with this hashtag, you'll show up when they do.

Industry conferences will usually have a hashtag that visitors can use to discuss the speakers, topics and anything else relating to the event. If you can contribute interesting ideas during these conferences, you'll be able to pick up some extra-targeted followers and join in with some conversations.

If you've got potential customers at the conference, you can publicise a special offer for delegates using a hashtag, and use it to collect leads. For example:

"Free #socialmedia audits for visitors to the #thebusinessshow2016 Retweet this message then click here: exposureninja.com/review"

This takes no time to set up, is completely free and can generate a good level of interest if the offer matches the audience well. It is however important to know that hashtags do not work on all social media platforms. Twitter and Instagram are great channels to use specific hashtags to boosts visibility, Facebook and PInterest also uses hashtags but quite differently than Twitter/Instagram.

We'll look at using Hashtags to boost your post visibility in more detail later on in the Twitter, Facebook, Pinterest and Instagram sections.

Turning Website Traffic Into Followers

One of the most frustrating sights is a business with tons of quality website traffic but a puny social media following. Some websites bury any sign of social media, so visitors have to embark on a superhuman detective hunt to become a follower.

The starting point is making sure your social icons are prominent on your website. This sounds basic, but when we're reviewing or consulting we'll sometimes notice that people have to scroll right to the bottom of the page before they see any social icons. The trouble is that only 2% of people actually get to the website footer, so immediately 98% of your visitors have no chance of converting to a follower.

If something is important on your website, the best place to put it is close to the top. If you maintain your social pages regularly and want to maximise follower numbers, you might want to put your social icons in your site's header with a call to action: "Follow us for tips, tricks and offers".

Some businesses choose to have live social feed widgets on their site. Facebook's Page Plugin gives you a piece of embed code for your website that shows a section of your Facebook page: cover photo, like button, recent posts and friends who like the page. Twitter's 'Widgets' do the same for your Twitter page, and whilst Instagram doesn't currently have a page widget, you can embed Insta posts on your site using its embed code (Wordpress users can embed an Instagram post just by pasting its URL on a new line in a post or page, and the IG post itself will automatically appear in place of the link), or third party plugins.

'Like Gates' and Discounts for Likes

A 'like gate' or 'social locker' is a device that requires someone to like or share something in order to get access to content on a page. Let's imagine that you have some instructional content that teaches your website visitors how to do something. You can either give this away free, or you could force visitors to 'pay' for the content by doing something social: like your page, follow you, Retweet or share. Plugins like Social Locker for Wordpress hide content on your site so that it's only revealed once the reader takes one of your desired actions.

If you've got really appealing bait in your locker, you'll find that people will readily comply. You can require them to Retweet a link to that page in order to gain access, and this will multiply your traffic as some of their followers and copy as they have done.

E-commerce sites can use 'discount for likes' strategies to offer savings to customers in return for Facebook likes. There are two main varieties here:

1. Cumulative likes: In this first example, a particular product will have a like counter showing a target number of likes. Once the product's likes have reached the target, a discount is 'unlocked' for everyone. Radykal's Discount for Likes Wordpress plugin lets you set different like targets for each product on your site, and can be a good way to encourage people to share your products with friends and those likely to increase the like count. Our advice is to initially set the target low, and keep raising it every time the target is met. Being the

first of 500 likes is less likely to initiate a share than if you're the 493rd and you just need to get 7 friends to comply.

2. Individual likes. In this scenario, shoppers are offered a discount in return for liking your page. Some plugins will appear in your shopping cart during checkout and offer you the chance to get a quick discount in return for a like, whilst Like 2 Discount by Laborator offers shoppers a discount code in return for first liking and second submitting their email address. This approach counters 'no code bounce' from shoppers that see a discount code box but, without having a code to use, wonder if they are about to pay too much and decide to leave.

Promoting Your Social Pages Using Email

Every email your business sends out can be an invitation to the recipient to like and follow your pages. In your signature you might want to include a call to action and links to each of your social profiles so that those who feel the benefit of their communication with you will engage.

We decided to make social media engagement part of our automated email stream. Once a visitor to www.exposureninja.com/review has requested their free website and marketing review, our email system follows up with them to make sure they received their review okay. If they did, an email asks them if they wouldn't mind taking the time to leave a review on our Facebook page. Whist not everyone does, it's a good way to get engagement from those that found the review most useful.

If you send out informative and useful broadcast emails (good job) or self-promotional newsletters (really? Still?), you can embed Tweets and posts in these. Sharing a particularly useful stat? Why not mention that it was something you posted on Facebook this week and give a link to the page for your readers to find more useful stats like this.

Embedding Social Media In Your Blog Posts

You might have noticed that it's now incredibly popular to embed social posts in blogs. With Facebook, Twitter and Instagram all making it easy to embed a Tweet, post or picture, embeds are a good way to keep your post interesting and varied whilst illustrating a point or showing someone's opinion on the topic. We'll look at how to make your blogging awesome in the next section.

Timing your posts

It's been said that *the difference between salad and garbage is timing*, and the same is true for social media. It's logical that you'd want to post at the times your audience is most active, so how do you know when that is?

Most business post on social while they are at work. But unfortunately this isn't always the most productive time to be active.

Generally the rule is that people don't check social media when they are fully engaged with work. Monday morning is a notorious dead zone, whilst Friday afternoon is working week peak time for social interactions. Recently Facebook announced that their own measure of communication sentiment, the 'happiness index', was 10% higher on Friday. A study by social media app Buffer found that Facebook posts and Tweets received better engagement on Thursdays, Fridays and, in particular, at the weekend. The effect on B2C weekend Twitter posting was most pronounced, with a 32% increase in engagement over the weekend.

One thing that needs emphasising is the difference in visibility algorithms between each network and how these can affect post timing. All the networks started life treating all posts equally: when you open Instagram, the feed you see is a list of posts from people you follow, ordered by the time they posted them. In other words it's recency that defines visibility. With Facebook on the other hand, what you see is a personalised list of posts based on Facebook's visibility algorithm (which we'll look at in more detail later). You might see a photo of a close friend's engagement ring from three days ago next to a post from five minutes ago. Twitter *used* to use recency only, although now shows 'While You Were Away' Tweets that have been selected by Twitter's algorithm for their estimated importance to you.

Algorithms. Great. What does it mean?

The difference in visibility algorithms explains why each network behaves differently, and why many businesses have a significantly larger following on one network compared to the others.

To be highly visible on Twitter for example, you have to post a lot. If you don't, people won't see your Tweets as they get buried in the stream of posts. Peter Bray from Moz found that after eighteen minutes, your Tweet was 'over the hill' for engagement. So frequency needs to be high, but how high are we talking? Socialbakers found that response per Tweet peaked at five Tweets per day. If that sounds disappointingly low to Twitter addicts out there, fear not: Track Social found that you could take your Tweet frequency to thirty per day whilst still increasing profile engagement. Clearly that's not going to be manageable for most small and medium-sized businesses, so we've found that two to five times per day is optimal to get the most bang for your buck

Meanwhile on Facebook, that sort of frequency isn't as important as the *engagement* level your posts attract. Another study from Socialbakers found that the most successful brands on Facebook tended to post five to ten times per week, and that this is around that sweet spot between keeping connected and becoming annoying. Bear in mind that Facebook visibility is a lot more reliant on engagement with your content. If your posts attract lots of likes and shares, they'll be seen by more people because Facebook's algorithm rewards high engagement posts with better 'reach'. If you constantly post content which gets low engagement (e.g. 'look at us' type posts), your post visibility will decrease and the invisibility/low-engagement downward spiral will accelerate.

Of course you're going to want to experiment and find out what timings works best for your audience. Across our clients we've found that before 9am and after 7pm can work really well for some e-commerce businesses who aim to get people outside of work hours, whilst midday can be a good time for B2B service companies as their audience checks their social feeds over lunch.

Premium social media management tools like Buffer can help you build an optimal schedule by suggesting times that engagement has historically been highest for you, and scheduling your posts to go out at these times each day. Alternatively you can schedule your posts through Facebook manually and measure engagement days and times through Facebook Insights, which we'll look at shortly.

The Networks In Depth

Every network has its own quirks, audience habits and etiquette, and they are there to be used to your advantage. In this section of the book we'll have a look at each social network in more detail and deconstruct the components of a successful campaign on each.

Facebook

Its 1.5 billion users make Facebook the number one social network on the planet. Compared to the number of businesses we talk to that say "our business would never work on Facebook," the number that *actually* don't work on Facebook is low. There are some businesses that it's just not the right platform for (dating websites generally have a tough time, after all people might not necessarily feel comfortable about being publicly associated with them), but in general if your customer are using Facebook for business or pleasure, you want to be seen there.

It's a mistake to assume that just because your business sells B2B and doesn't have the most exciting product in the world, that you won't do well on Facebook. Guess what, your customers still spend their spare moments checking Facebook - it hasn't got to 1.5 billion users just by targeting colleges and universities. Your customers think about your market in their spare time and they want to keep up-to-date so they remain good at their jobs, so let's make sure they're seeing your message. "But none of our competitors are on Facebook." Good!

For B2C companies and impulse purchases, Facebook can be a goldmine. We're finding ourselves recommending it as THE main marketing channel for an increasing number of industries — even over Google. The Facebook advertising platform continues to grow and evolve, and offers better targeting, cheaper clicks and more audience insights. If you're not already paying Facebook a lot of attention (and a lot of money) then get excited, because there is so much potential here.

Profitable Facebook Marketing

Any Facebook campaign starts with your business page. And yes, you need a business page not a personal page. To engage with personal pages fully, people need to add them as a friend, and very few people will add a business as a friend. If you don't already have a business page, first you'll need a personal page and then you can go to https://www.facebook.com/pages/create to set up your page.

If you would like a step-by-step walkthrough of how to set up a Facebook page, go to www.profitablesocialmediamarketing.com and sign up for the free social media video course. For now we'll look at some of the main components of a good Facebook business page.

The Perfect Profile Photo

It's easy to overthink things here. Your profile photo should be your logo in a square format. Hopefully your logo has at least a couple of colours and is easily recognisable from a small thumbnail image.

Check out how Nutella's local UK page (https://www.facebook.com/nutellauk) uses a colourful illustration of a Nutella jar to make their profile photo more interesting, whilst keeping the familiar logo prominent.

Cover Photo

The most effective cover photos instantly communicate one or more of the reasons people like your business or products. When someone lands on the page, this image is your chance to stir up those feelings and reinforce the benefits of what you do.

Notice how Tough Mudder (muddy assault courses with a team focus) plays on the participation and teamwork angle in its cover photo here:

While St Jude Children's Hospital seeks to elicit an emotional response from their very well designed cover image, with a nod to a call to action:

E-commerce sites can use their cover photo to showcase their products with pictures that effectively communicate the voice of their brand. Whether it's women's fashion etailer Missguided, pushing their partying and attitude:

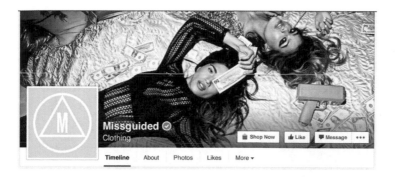

Or menswear subscription service Trunk Club focusing more on the rugged yet classic:

These cover images all do a good job of selling the benefits of the business, even if they don't always explicitly state them. They're also all good quality: no pixelated and stretched logos, strange crops or key elements of the image cut off by the profile photo. Sounds basic, and it is — people spend social media time looking at attractive things.

Description sections

There are plenty of different widget areas available on your Facebook page: about description, opening hours, address, contact details, reviews, reviews, photos, apps, videos, visitor posts, upcoming events, polls and notes. The sections you choose to show should be guided by the information your visitors are looking for when they land on your page. Local businesses will want to prioritise opening hours and location information, whereas businesses heavy on visuals might choose to make photos and videos most prominent.

But whatever your business, writing a concise summary at the top in your 'About' section is crucial. This is where you deliver cupid's arrow straight into your visitors' hearts with a benefits-laden description of what you do and why you're different. Don't be fooled by the fact we're on social media - this description area is crucial sales copy to sell your page and business.

Here's a very good description from Whole Foods London: *"Fresh eats and inspiring posts from our 7 Whole Foods Market stores. We sell foods with no artificial ingredients — feel good about where you shop!"*

In one sentence they've packed 3 benefit statements. We have a key benefit of the product (no artificial ingredients); of the page (fresh eats and inspiring posts), and of buying from Whole Foods (feel good about where you shop).

Here's another **great** description, this time from Fannie May Chocolates: *"For over 95 years Fannie May has produced fine quality gourmet chocolates that have become a family tradition all across the world."* They've used authority (95 years), positioning (family tradition) and a benefit (fine quality, gourmet). They also have a KILLER mission statement: "The finest quality gourmet chocolates in the world." It's big, bold, attractive, and making me hungry.

Here's an example of a **bad** description: *"Welcome to the St. Jude Children's Research Hospital Facebook page. Before you post, please review our posting policy located on the About page."* Their only call to action is to review terms and conditions. We praised them for their profile and cover photo, but unfortunately it looks like the legal team got their way when it came to the copy.

Here's another **bad** description from another company we praised for their profile and cover photo, Nutella: *"Welcome to the UK & Ireland Nutella page! Current fan count 1,032,515."* Seriously? Zero benefits or appeal, and the fan count is out of date by a factor of *thirty*. It just goes to show that no one gets it right 100% of the time.

Tough Mudder took the approach of filming a promotional video which they've used in their about section:

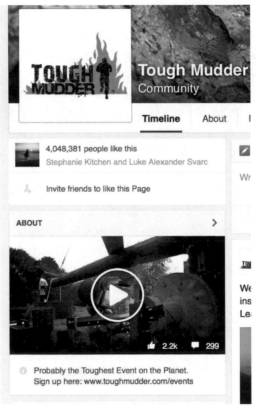

Importantly they've used a snappy text description as well (and a good one at that), because not everyone is going to watch the video.

The general rule for Facebook (and indeed all the social networks) is that you want to make your profile pages as complete as possible. Like an attractive shop window, it makes your business look active and exciting, and increases the likelihood of people interacting with you. It also gives Google more content to index, raising the chances of your page showing up prominently in search results. We've found that more complete pages tend to show up more often across Facebook too, although whether this is due to higher engagement statistics or because Facebook rewards this completion remains to be seen.

Updating Company History

If your company has a long history, Facebook's Timeline can be a good way to introduce this in a way that's gentle without forcing it on those who don't care. Check out how US Outdoor clothing company L.L Bean uses their Facebook timeline history on their page https://www.facebook.com/llbean, which goes right back to 1912. You'll notice that, other than the timeline, they don't really talk a lot about how old the company is, because *most* people just don't care — they want good products now, not 100 years ago. But undoubtedly there *is* a section of customers to whom history is an important part of what makes L.L. Bean different.

If your company has history and you want to include important dates in your Facebook timeline, just create a post as you would normally, and click the clock icon to set the date and time of your post. You can then choose the year, month, day and even hour and minute that you want the post to show up as.

What Sort Of Content Should You Post?

Usually when a business hasn't made much headway on Facebook, you'll notice that the majority of their posts are overtly self-promotional. They'll talk about their own services, post links to their website and share the occasional "10% off!" deals. It's all about as enticing as talking to a bad used car salesman on the last day of the month. People will avoid it like the plague because there's nothing in it for them. No one goes on Facebook to find out information about people's new websites, all they care about is getting closer to their goals, having fun and feeling significant. So that's what your content should do for them.

The simplest way to think about good Facebook page content is to treat your feed like a magazine. A magazine exists primarily to sell adverts, but a book of adverts won't get many readers. So the magazine publishers have articles to entice the reader and hold their attention long enough for them to read the ads. If the mixture is too ad-heavy, readership goes down. A profitable Facebook business page seeks to strike exactly the same balance: it gives people enough useful, interesting or entertaining content to keep them interested for the commercial messages.

The Innocent Drinks Facebook page (https://www.facebook.com/innocent.drinks/) finds a great balance. A mixture of jokes and entertaining pictures balances the sales messages nicely, and even these sales messages are positioned in an entertaining way:

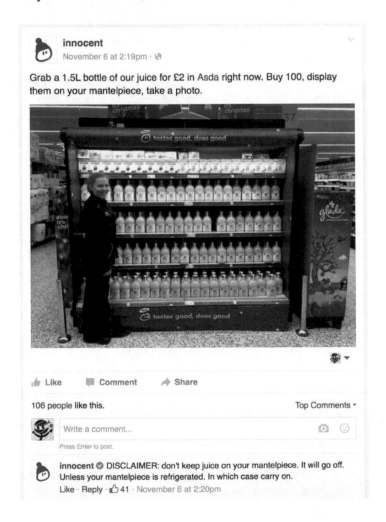

Notice how the first comment immediately reestablishes their fun and quirky personality, and kick started the conversation with their audience.

Posts that reinforce your business's uniqueness or differentiation can be both entertaining *and* promotional. Notice how Savills Barbers in Sheffield differentiate themselves on Facebook with professional quality photos of their team in action. Their personality comes through in the posts, and they get a fantastic response because of the extra effort they put in:

This quality of content elevates the perception of their business far above any of their local competitors. Sharing photos of haircuts, behind the scenes banter and 'day in the life' videos means that they've acquired 60,000 Facebook fans, and trainees flock to their training academy from around the world. It just goes to show the power of doing something different and committing to showing a high quality face on Facebook.

Facebook Page Apps

In addition to Facebook's standard business page functionality, you can add apps that allow visitors to do a bit more from your page. Before we dive in and take a look at the different types of App available, let's look at how these apps are shown on a Facebook page:

You'll see how the Timeline | About | Photos | Giveaway | More banner shown underneath the cover photo stretches to just over half of the page, and that only 5 tabs are visible without clicking More. This means that those extra tabs are almost invisible, so it's crucial that your visible tabs are the most compelling, because the non-visible apps will get barely any engagement.

To add an app to your page you first need to search it by name. Let's go through the process to add the static HTML/Iframe app to your page, as this is one of the most popular (we'll look at what it does in just a minute).

First you need to search for "Static HTML" in the Facebook search bar. You'll see that the name of the app shows up:

Clicking on it brings up the app page:

Click to add static HTML to a page and choose your page from the drop down menu:

Click Add Page Tab, then on the next screen click to Set Up Tab. You'll then see the settings for that page tab:

In the static HTML tab, you can put code and text that you want to show up on your Facebook page. This is useful if you want to add a form (contact form or signup form) or some content (for example testimonials) to the new tab on your page. You'll notice that by default the tab is named 'Welcome', but you can change this by clicking the Actions drop down menu and choosing Edit Name and Image.

You can remove apps from your page by doing the following:

First, from your page click Settings and then Apps from the left hand menu:

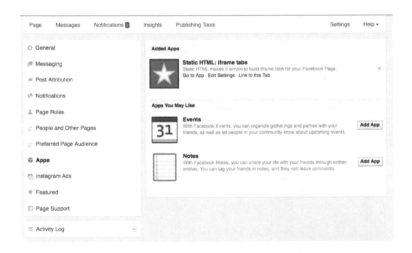

Click the X mark next to any apps that you want to remove from your page. Note that if you manage multiple pages, this will remove it ONLY from the page that you are currently managing.

Also note that if you are using Facebook Business Manager, you will need to click 'Use Facebook as my page' to get access to the search box to find new apps.

Now let's look at finding some tabs and apps to add to your page. The ones that you choose for your page will obviously depend on your business type and the goal of your page. The process for setting up each new tab varies slightly according to the tab's functionality, but it's usually extremely straightforward as the app itself guides you through the setup process. We're not going to take you step by step through the process of setting up each of the apps mentioned in this section, but if you have any questions or need any help then of course you can get in touch with us through our website www.ExposureNinja.com, and we'll be happy to help.

Here are some of the main app categories:

Facebook App Category 1: Lead Capture & Contact Forms

At Exposure Ninja we're big fans of building a nice solid email list. Building an audience on social media is awesome, but owning those contact details yourself in an email list means that when the social tides change (and it's a case of *when* not *if*), you're not left starting from scratch on a new platform with no audience. With a well-presented lead capture form on your Facebook page, you can give visitors the chance to provide their contact details in exchange for a gift, promo code or taster.

Aweber and Mailchimp are the two email list providers that we recommend most often, and both have handy Facebook apps that you can install on your page. You'll need an Aweber/Mailchimp account first, but once you're ready to install the app search Facebook for "Aweber" or "Mailchimp" and choose the APP result, not the Business Page.

For other email list managers (such as Infusionsoft) you can add a form by copying the form code into the Static HTML Facebook app we looked at above.

The name that you give your lead capture form app is crucial. Call it something attractive (Free Guide to X, Discount Voucher, Free Delivery Code etc.) and you'll get people clicking on it:

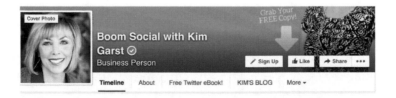

Here you can see Kim has called her lead capture form "Free Twitter eBook", so no prizes for guessing who she's trying to attract and the bait she's offering. She knows the score.

Facebook App Category 2: Social Media Page Apps

As if having so many different types of app wasn't confusing enough, how about embedding one social media page inside another? With apps like Iconosquare (for Instagram), Tabsite (for Pinterest), and with YouTube and Twitter's own apps, you can have feeds from these social networks showing up inside a tab on your Facebook page.

This is particularly important if your social media work has focused on one of the other networks and you want to make the most of that momentum and attention on Facebook too.

To add one of these apps (for example YouTube), search Facebook for "YouTube" and look for the YouTube app in the search results. If you don't see it, click "Find More Search Results For YouTube", then choose Apps from the sidebar. You'll notice that there are a number of different YouTube Apps for Pages, and it's usually the one with the most monthly active users that you want.

Facebook App Category 3: Online Booking

If you want to allow your customers to book appointments with you through your Facebook page, there are a range of apps that allow this, such as Schedulicity and Appointy. These types of service will require you to use their appointment booking software, which is rarely free with the exception of SetMore that actually has a meaningful free plan.

Facebook App Category 4: E-commerce Stores

Yes, you can build an entire store right inside your Facebook page. Now this won't be a *replacement* for your own website store (or any Amazon or Ebay stores you have), but if you use an e-commerce platform that has simple integration with Facebook then it can be very simple to set up.

Platforms that offer this type of integration include Shopify and Volusion, and there are plenty of apps that work with Magento and Wordpress.

Facebook App Category 5: Contest Apps

Contests drive engagement, and the more engagement your pages and posts get, the more visible they become across Facebook. From quizzes and sweepstakes to games and photo contests, there are plenty of things you can do with visitors to your Facebook page to get them interacting.

Pagemodo, Contest Domination and (Ninja favourite) Rafflecopter all have Facebook contest apps that allow you to give prizes away to your audience who compete by submitting photos, liking, visiting or commenting on your page. For all of these services, you'll first need to create an account and set up your contest on their site. Then, once you install their companion Facebook app, you can make the contest visible through your Facebook page.

One tip which sounds obvious but warrants repeating is to make sure your prize is genuinely appealing to the audience you want to attract to your page. It can be tempting (particularly for businesses with a high-ticket product or service) to give away something small and unrelated with mass appeal. But whilst offering shopping vouchers or Amazon gift certificates as a prize can attract a lot of entries, they won't generate you the sort of highly engaged visitors you're looking for. Each time your page likes get 'diluted' by an untargeted audience, your engagement statistics will drop and your page content will become less visible as a result.

Don't forget that you don't *need* a contest app to run a simple contest on your Facebook page though. Making a post that asks your audience to vote, like or comment is all within Facebook's promotions Terms & Conditions. If a simple contest is all you're after, this can save you time and money.

We'll often outreach to bloggers and owners of successful Facebook pages and offer them a free prize to give away in a contest to their audience. They get the engagement that comes from running the contest, and they tend to pick some extra likes as a result of offering a free prize. We get exposure to their audience for the product given as a prize, and will pick up sales from the contest as a result of people seeing the product, loving it and buying it when they didn't win.

The Diary Of A Jewellery Lover Blog
Product/Service · 4,009 Likes · August 17 · Edited ·

Like Page ▾

To win a set of 12 pretty battery operated tealight candles by
http://www.pkgreenshop.co.uk
Simply like this post and comment to enter.
If you are feeling generous like my page and pop over to
https://www.facebook.com/pkgreenuk?fref=ts and like their page too.
Remember sharing is caring
Ends 10am 31st August 2015

312 Likes · 387 Comments · 250 Shares

👍 Like   💬 Comment   ➤ Share

In this contest we reached out to the owner of *The Diary Of A Jeweler Lover Blog* and offered them a set of LED candles, stocked by an e-commerce client of ours. She ran this post directly from her Facebook page, which attracted over 300, likes, almost 400 comments and 250 shares. The product was not expensive and our client got thousands of qualified impressions in return.

As you can see, there is plenty of potential to turn your Facebook page into something a little bit more dynamic than the typical business page. One thing we've learned is that there are no hard and fast rules, and every audience is slightly different in their preferences and engagement habits. It'll be up to you to experiment and find the sort of topics, apps and content that generates the most attention.

Why Is My Reach So Low? Facebook Visibility Explained

As more businesses wake up to the opportunity that Facebook presents, the volume of content that is being published on the network continues to accelerate. Imagine the amount of information that is being shared by Facebook's 1.5+ billion active users (it's more than 300 *petabytes* worth, incidentally)!

As people share content with more friends and pages, the competition for each position in the News Feed continues to increase. This has led to changes in post distribution, including a decline in organic reach for content posted by Pages. Facebook has argued that their goal is to provide more relevant content to each person, based on how they engage with the content that is provided in their News Feed and overall on Facebook. They've stated: "as part of an ongoing survey, we asked hundreds of thousands of people how they feel about the content in they News Feeds. People told us they want to see more stories from friends and pages they care about, and less promotional content." As a result of these studies, in 2014 Facebook announced that they would penalise brand content. In short, they recognised that individuals didn't want to be constantly pestered by companies like you and I trying to sell them something. Facebook then **limited** the reach of organic promotional posts, such as those pushing a product or service, telling people to install an app, or asking people to enter contest with no real context. In other words, Facebook decided that if you want to constantly promote your business to its users — even if they like and follow you — fewer of them would see your posts.

But do these changes mean that organic reach on Facebook is dead? Of course not! All this just means that those of us who want potential customers to continue seeing our messages have to be more creative and make sure that our posts are actually *engaging,* rather than purely promotional. It also means that we'll almost certainly end up giving Facebook some money to ensure that we get the

136

visibility that we're used to, but that's no bad thing considering the opportunity it presents.

Of course the silver lining to all of this is that your competitors likely won't have changed their strategy at all. They'll continue posting self-promotional links to their websites and being invisible to their audience. All these changes do is force individuals, brands and businesses to ditch their lazy (and ineffective) marketing tactics of "10% OFF TODAY ONLY!!!!" and think outside the box, creating and posting content that their fans and potential fans will actually like, share and comment on.

You might have noticed that unless you already have a very dedicated fan base, only posted engaging content will not be enough. This is where paying a small amount of money to boost your posts can get things started and begin to build you higher engagement levels. At this point, many people usually argue: "well I don't have a budget!" It is a common misconception that large sums of money need to be invest into advertising when in fact a budget of around USD$100 per month (or even less) can go a long way IF (and only if) you know your ideal customer (remember our section about customer personas?) so that you can target them in Facebook ads.

Verifying Your Page

You might have noticed that some business pages have a blue tick next to the page name. This means that they've been verified, and gives them better visibility in search results. To verify your page, click Settings -> Page Verification. You'll have the option to verify by automated phone call or by sending Facebook copies of business utility bills or incorporation documents. Once you submit these, Facebook's team will verify your details to make sure they match public records and you should be good to go!

Facebook Analytics

If you struggled in the customer persona section to identify your perfect audience, the good news is that Facebook actually *wants* to help you. Insights is an analytics tool that allows you to measure and track various metrics, from the number of likes your page attracts each day to the number of people seeing and engaging with your posts. But before we dive into Insights, let's look at the main metrics that we have at our disposal:

Reach: The number of people your ad was served to.
Impressions: each time an ad is shown to a user, regardless of whether the user clicks or takes any other action on the ad.

Frequency: the average number of times your ad was served to each person.

CTR (Click-Through Rate): the number of clicks your ads received divided by the number of times you ad is shown on the site (impressions) in the same time period.

CPC (Cost per Click): A type of campaign pricing where you pay each time someone clicks on your ad. This is the best type of campaign pricing to use when you want to drive specific action on your website or Facebook page.

CPM (Cost per Thousand Impressions): a type of campaign pricing where you pay based on the number of people who view your ad. This is the best type of campaign pricing to use if you want to raise general awareness of your business within a targeting audience

Page Likes: the number of likes on your page.

Page Engagement: The number of actions related to the Page and your Page's post — actions can include shares, likes, clicks and comments.

Post Likes: the number of likes on your page's post.

Post Engagement: the number of actions related to your Page's post — actions can include shares, likes, clicks and comments.

Post Shares: the number of shares of your page's post.

Pages to Watch: Facebook provides you with similar types of businesses pages, which helps you compare the performance of your page with your competitors.

Website Clicks: the number of clicks on links appearing in your post or page that directed people to your sites off Facebook.

Landing Page: it is a web page that appears in response to clicking on an advertisement. It can be a Facebook Page, an App or even an external URL.

Clicks to play video: the number of clicks to play video.

Video views: the number of times your video was viewed for **3 seconds or more.**

Custom audiences: upload a list of email addresses or phone numbers of at least 100 people and Facebook will deliver the ad to those people if they're on Facebook. You can also build audiences from people that visit your website or who have used your mobile app.

Lookalike audience: help you reach people who are similar to your current customers for fan acquisition, website registration, off-Facebook purchases, coupon claims and brand awareness.

Conversion tracking: helps businesses measure the return on investment on their Facebook Ads by reporting on the actions people take after viewing those ads: checkouts, registrations, leads, key page views, adds to cart. Etc.

Conversion value: The total revenue returned from conversation or Facebook credit spends that occurred your website or app.

Now that we've covered the definitions, let's dive in to see what Insights looks like.

The first tab is the Overview. At the top the page you will see the date range of the data you're looking at. There is a way to choose your own date range, but more on that later.

There are three little boxes underneath that are pretty self-explanatory: Page Likes (the number of people who have liked your page within that date range), Post Reach (the number of people who have seen your posts) and Engagement (the number of people that have Likes, Comment, Shared or Clicked on your posts). Below the boxes you will have an overview of your most recent posts: the type, targeting, reach, engagement etc. Although all the tabs should be explored, two of them are a little more important that the rest.

The "Posts" tab allows you to see the peak times that your fans are online. For this data alone we would happily bow at the feet of Facebook because it means that you can synchronise your posting schedule to match when your audience are most likely to see your posts. In "Post Types" you can see whether videos, links or photos work best on your page and resonate more with your audience.

The second most useful tab is the "People" tab that gives you a rundown of exactly who is visiting your page, whether is it predominantly male or female, the age range and also their location. This can help you identify *who* your Facebook audience is, and whether the content you're sharing is hitting the right notes with your chosen demographics.

If you want to do an in-depth analysis of your Facebook page including the daily, weekly and/or monthly reach, impressions or engagement then you need to export the information. At the top right of your page you'll see "Export". Click on that and choose whether you would like Page data (key metrics for engagement, like sources and audience details), Post data (key post metrics for reach, impressions and feedback) or Video data (key video metrics including view, unique views, page views and organic views). Select the date range and whether you would like to export it in an .xls or .csv file. You will mostly likely export the Page data Excel file, which will give you information regarding new likes, engagement, impressions and reach.

Facebook (and Instagram) Ads

Pages upon pages can be written about Facebook ads. In fact, at Exposure Ninja we have dedicated Ninjas who spend huge amounts of time squeezing, tweaking and optimising Facebook, LinkedIn, Twitter and Instagram posts for our clients. But let's have a look at some of the key features that make Facebook one of the most useful advertising platforms for small businesses, and walk through the process of getting an ad campaign set up. You'll notice that we have added Instagram to this chapter because Facebook has made it incredibly easy to boost posts in ads manager to both Facebook and Instagram simultaneously. But more about that in a bit!

To get started with Facebook ads, visit https://www.facebook.com/ads/manage. This is Facebook's Ads Manager, and is the friendly face of Facebook advertising. There is a more advanced editor called Power Editor that allows you to create 'dark' posts and Instagram ads, but we'll look at that later. From the ads manager, click "Create Ads" to be directed to another page that asks your to choose your objective. The most popular objectives are "Boost post", "Promote your page", "Send people to your website" and "Increase conversion on your website." So which one will it be? First, let's look at the simplest and most common type of Facebook Ad, the boosted post.

Boosted Post Ads

Boosting a post allows you to give it some extra visibility by paying to have it seen by more people than would see it if you relied on regular 'organic' visibility.

To get started boosting a post, head to Facebook Ads Manager and click "Boost your post". You'll need to choose your page and pick the post you want to boost. Then you'll enter the Ad Set where you will define your audience, budget and schedule.

Audience targeting on Facebook is an art unto itself, so let's start with the basics:

Location: Which geographies do you want to focus on? You can go as broad as adding every country in the list or as narrow as focusing on a specific city and a radius around that city. If you're a multinational/multi-currency e-commerce site, you'll want to set up different Ad Sets for each different currency so that you can show the native currency to each audience, and direct them to the page on your site showing that currency.

Age: How old is your target audience? If you're unsure, set the age range broad and then check back in 48 hours to see which age groups are responding best to your ads, so that you can double down into that audience.

Gender: Are you focusing only on men/women or both? If you notice from Facebook Insights that 76% of your engagement comes from women, consider targeting your ads at only women even if your product or service is not gender-specific. Remember that Facebook rewards ads that get high engagement, so you generally want to do all you can to target your ads to those who are the most likely to respond.

Languages: What languages does your target audience speak?

You will notice a little button that says "More Demographics." This is when it gets interesting (or

145

creepy, depending what your attitude to Facebook's user data capture is)!

Relationship: Are your audience interested in a specific gender? Are you targeting only married individuals?

Education: Does your target audience have a specific level of education? Did they study a specific field? Maybe they attended a specific school? The range of schools is pretty limited for now, but Facebook is adding new ones all the time.

Work: Do they work for a specific company or maybe hold a certain title that you would be interested in targeting? Be aware that this will significantly limit your audience size, but if your offering is really only relevant for a particular job type then this focus can save you a lot of your ad budget.

Additional targeting options include home, ethnic affinity, generation, parents, politics (US) and life events. This is why it is extremely important to understand your customer persona as Facebook advertising allows you to be very specific in your targeting.

Next are Interests. You can be as specific as you like here. For example instead of writing Opera, look for the specific opera that they might be interested in.

146

Following interests, you can choose the specific behaviours of their target audience: reach people based on their purchase behaviors or intent, device usage and more. Some behavior data is available for US audiences only, but Facebook are constantly rolling out more targeting options to give us advertisers more choice than ever about who we want to reach.

Last is Connections, which allows you to reach people who have a specific kind of connection to your Page, app or event. This will narrow your audience to include only people with that specific connection who also meet the other targeting categories you've selected.

This is a lot of information to process in one go, so let's do an exercise.

Problem: 'The Ninjas' is an adrenaline-fuelled musical that combines elements of love, loss and digital marketing in a 90-minute emotional rollercoaster that leaves audiences (literally) speechless. The show is run in 4 different countries (U.S, Canada, France and England), and the production company wants to use Facebook to increase awareness. Their objective/goal is not specifically to sell tickets but first to raise awareness about the show, which will lead to word of mouth, and then to sales. The production company has started a Facebook page, perfected their voice/tone and have their ideal customer persona. They have created beautiful content that is being currently shared organically and, although they have a little bit of engagement, they want to invest in Facebook advertising.

Solution: As the shows are located in four specific countries, we would obviously start boosting visibility in those areas first. The long-term goal is worldwide awareness, but with the show still limited to four countries we can expand the campaign to neighbouring countries later.

The targeting that will be most useful here is Interests. As The Ninjas is a musical, we might target: Men and Females who speak English, that are aged between 25 - 50 and located in U.S, Canada, France and England. We'll also make sure that they are interested in other types of show that are somewhat similar to The Ninjas. If it were ballet, we would do the same with other types of ballet.

Our final targeting might look like this:

Location: *US, Canada, England, France*
Age: *25 - 50*
Gender: *ALL*
Languages: *English*
Interests: *Cats, Les Miserables, La Cage aux Folles, Annie, Rent, Chicago, The Phantom of the Opera, Evita, Wicked, Cabarets, Carousel, Beauty and the Beast, Hairspray, the Producers, Grease.*

Choosing Boosted Post Budget

When deciding how much you want to spend on a boosted post, bear in mind that you're going to be experimenting and tweaking your post and audience over time, so we tend to recommend starting at a manageable level and scaling up once you have a formula that works.

Next you must choose how you want Facebook to optimise the delivery of your ad: by post engagement (getting the maximum number of likes, shares and comments at the lowest cost), impressions (have your ad seen as many times as possible) and daily unique reach (deliver your ads to as many different people as possible). Unless you know your site's exact conversion rate and have a strict cost per acquisition limit, we would recommend clicking automatic. Choose when you get charged (per impression or post engagement — usually you want start with per post engagement, unless your ad attracts a lot of clicks), your ad scheduling and delivery type. Last, name your Ad Set and click: Choose Ad Creative.

Instagram automatically pops up in this section, which means that you can boost the same post on Facebook and Instagram (with the same targeting) at the same the time. Other than the Instagram option you will see three other boosting possibilities: Desktop Right Column, Mobile News Feed and Desktop News Feed.

We would recommend keeping mobile and desktop (unless your audience is primarily on mobile) and remove Desktop Right Column, as boosted posts don't tend to do well here. You will always have better success on Instagram with an ad designed specifically for Instagram, so it's usually best to avoid promoting boosted posts here.

Click Place Order and you're done. Well, almost...

Your post needs to be approved, which usually takes 15 minutes. If your post isn't approved, there could be a number of reasons why but the most common is the 20% text rule. To prevent Facebook looking too ad-y, their Advertising Policies state that the image used in an ad cannot include more than 20% text. Facebook defines this as having text in 20% of the squares it adds as an overlay on top of your image. If in doubt, use the Facebook Grid Tool at https://www.facebook.com/ads/tools/text_overlay if your ad is not approved because of this problem, you will have to go back, re-edit the photo and re-submit everything again.

Facebook will also disapprove your ad will if your business promotes something that it doesn't allow ads for, such as tobacco products, weapons, drugs or dating websites. Luckily we're only marketing ninjas, because real ninjas would be severely limited in their paid ad options on Facebook.

PLEASE NOTE: once you have attached an ad to a post and the ad goes live, you can no longer edit the post. So make sure that there are no spelling or grammar errors before you launch. Once launched the only option you have if there is an error is to delete the whole post, and the ad, and start over.

Measuring Boosted Post Campaign Success

So your boosted post has finished running and engagement was great. You got some likes, comments, shares and plenty of traffic to your website. What's next? It's time to look at results of your campaign in the Ads Manager.

One of the key indicators of a post's success is that your cost per engagement should be low. A low cost means that you targeting incredibly well and a lot of people were engaging with that specific post. Facebook defines cost as the average you paid for each action associated with your objective.

If you want to start getting into the nitty-gritty you can look up things like: Breakdown by Delivery: age, gender, country, region, placement; Breakdown by action; Breakdown by time; Performance, Engagement etc. By looking at performance broken down by region we can see which country engaged the most and who was the cheapest to reach. This kind of information can feed into future campaigns, and even future decisions about territories to expand into.

Other Types of Facebook Advert

Whilst Boosted Posts are the most popular ad type thanks to their simplicity, there are more advanced (and usually more effective) strategies available to those that are willing to venture a little further inside…

Facebook's Power Editor is a more advanced ad management interface that gives you access to every Facebook advertising type. Once you're familiar with the layout, it allows for super quick management of your ads, but learning how to use the Power Editor takes a little longer than the Ads Manager. With its greater complexity comes control though, and for anyone that wants to get serious with Facebook advertising, Power Editor is worth spending some time getting to grips with.

To open up the Power Editor, head to https://www.facebook.com/ads/manage/powereditor

Here is what you will find:

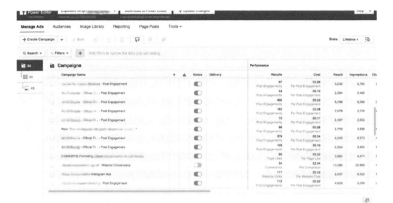

Along the top of the screen we have tabs for:

- **Manage Ads.** This is where you'll manage Ad Campaigns, Ad Sets and the Ads themselves
- **Audiences.** This is where you can create an audience to target in your ads, and where audiences that you've saved previously will show up. By creating and saving audiences, you can quickly run ads to the same group of people without having to go through all of the targeting options from scratch
- **Image Library.** Your ads will use images, and through this tab you can add and remove images and variations that you want to test.
- **Reporting.** You can create custom reports and have these automatically scheduled and emailed to you. Perfect if you don't have time to check your ads every day, but you want to be kept in the loop.
- **Page Posts.** This gives you quick access to all of the posts made, scheduled and promoted

from your page. Check their engagement statistics and create scheduled posts from here.
- **Tools.** This gives you access to Facebook Pixels (more on them in just a minute), Conversion Tracking setup, Account Settings and Billing.

For now we'll focus on the Manage Ads tab, as we can do what we need from here. Before we get stuck in though, let's talk about how Facebook Ads are structured.

On the left hand side of the screenshot above, you'll notice 3 vertical tabs.

These represent ad **Campaigns** (the top box), **Ad Sets** (second box down), and the **Adverts** themselves (bottom box). A **Campaign** represents a goal, for example: "Ninja Merchandise Product Sales". Underneath this campaign sits **Ad Sets**. These are groups of **adverts** that share common targeting. For example if, in my Ninja Merchandise Product Sales, I wanted to run separate Ads on Facebook to women and men, and another set of ads to Instagram users, I would have 3 Ad Sets:
1. Women on Facebook

154

2. Men on Facebook
3. Instagram users

Each of these ad sets would have different ads inside them targeting each audience.

If that's all as clear as mud to you, then fear not — let's go through the process of setting up a campaign, and it'll all start to make more sense.

First up, from the Power Editor click + Create Campaign. A box will appear:

Choose whether you want to use an existing campaign or create a new one. Choose an Ad Set or create a new one (remember that an Ad Set is a set of ads targeting a particular audience), and create your new Ad name.

Next up you'll see the main edit window:

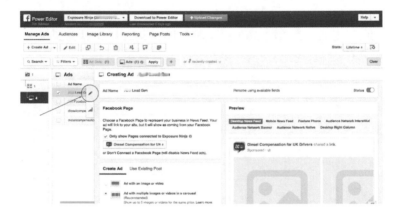

This is where you create the ad itself, from choosing the photos or videos to show, writing the ad copy, choosing the page that you want to link to and picking a Call to Action, to linking conversion tracking (which we'll look at shortly).

Exactly which options will be available to you on this page change almost daily as Facebook improves its ad platform, so we'll go through some general best

156

practice principles and sneak in some tips that we've found to boost conversions.

- Generally ads with multiple pictures in a carousel do better than ads with only one image, because they increase the likelihood that the viewer will see something that appeals to them. Your first image in a carousel should obviously be the most appealing, and if you're selling a product directly through the ads you'll want to show it from multiple angles or in multiple uses.
- Slideshow videos *sometimes* convert better than images, although we've found the difference too close to be statistically significant, so it's best to set up ads using both and test for yourself.
- If you're selling a product, which, on the surface, appears expensive for what it is, then it can be a good idea to mention the price in the ad copy — either in the headline or in the page description. This way you filter out price shoppers *before* they click (and you have to pay for that click). If they see the high price and *still* click, you know that they're qualified and your conversion rate *per click* will be better.
- When using a CTA button ('Shop Now', 'More Info') you'll lose most of your website description text, so make sure that any key

benefits are mentioned in the website title or in the text above the ad.

- In the descriptive text above the ad, test using questions such as "What do you think of the colour of this bag?" or "Who do you know that has been affected?" Questions such as these trigger answers in the viewer's mind, and if this answer is compelling enough to them they'll sometimes drop it into the comments. This is great because comments on your ads show Facebook that people are engaging, and increase the visibility (social reach) of your ads for no extra cost.
- Images that show a product in use tend to outperform 'studio' images, although again this is a massive generalisation across dozens of product types, so TEST to find the approach that works best for you.

Custom and Lookalike Audiences & The Facebook Pixel

Facebook has really outdone itself when focusing on the types of people that you can reach through advertising. We've talked about the basics of audience targeting, but Custom and Lookalike Audience allow us to go one step further with some seriously ninja targeting.

The Custom Audience feature allows you reach customers you already know with ads on Facebook. For example, let's say you have an epic email list that you have collected through your website over the years. Facebook will let you upload these email addresses to create a Custom Audience, and target these customers with Facebook ads if they are on Facebook. You can create custom audiences from emails, phone numbers, people that visit your website and/or from people who use your mobile app.

Creating a Custom Audience from emails and phone numbers is fairly simple. Once you're in Ads Manager, click Tools -> Audiences. There are three different types of audiences that you can create:

Custom Audiences: You can create a custom audience from your existing customer list, through your website traffic (using the Facebook pixel) or through your mobile app.

Lookalike Audiences: Reach new people who are *similar* to to the audience you've uploaded, have visited your website, or who like your page.

Saved Audience: This is where you can save your commonly used targeting options for easy reuse. Choose your demographics, interests, and behaviors, and then save them to reuse in future ads.

When creating a Custom Audience by uploading your customer list, Facebook matches emails, phone numbers, Facebook user IDs or mobile advertiser IDs to profiles on Facebook. The process is incredibly simple: either upload a file, copy and paste your custom list or import from MailChimp and voila!

The website traffic option allows you to create a list of people who have visited your website and/or visited specific web pages. The Facebook Pixel is a piece of code that you drop into your website which allows Facebook to track visitors to your website and register actions like forms filled in, or sales made (i.e. 'conversions'). This single-use pixel is not to be confused with the old conversion tracking pixel or custom audience pixels, which are to be phased out. This new Facebook Pixel can be used for both building custom audiences and tracking conversions.

There are two main benefits of using the Facebook pixel for conversion tracking with your Facebook ads. Firstly, it enables you to accurately find your CPA, or 'Cost Per Acquisition'. This is the amount of money that you have to spend with Facebook in order to get that sale, contact form submission or other action. By tracking CPAs of each of your sources of revenue, you can easily compare Return on Investment (ROI) for each of your marketing channels. You might find that Facebook brings you a new customer for £3, whilst Google Adwords costs £10 to generate each customer.

Having this data means you can make rational decisions about where best to put your advert spend, and is crucial to expand a campaign profitably.

The second benefit of using conversion tracking is that when Facebook knows what sort of audience is converting, their algorithms can find more of that audience, create a Custom Audience and serve your ad to them. It could, for example, take an e-commerce site a while to identify that most of their buyers were a particular demographic. By running a Facebook ad campaign optimised for conversions, however, Facebook might discover this bias much quicker, and automatically increase your visibility with this target audience in order to generate you the most conversions for your budget.

Here is how to create a Facebook Pixel:
1. Create your pixel in Ads Manager. Click Tools - > Pixels -> Facebook Pixel -> Create Pixel. Enter the name for your pixel. There is only one pixel per ad account so choose a name that represents your business! Click Create Pixel.
2. Add the pixel to your website. If you work on your website yourself, click Install Pixel Now and if you someone else works on your website, click Email Pixel Code -> Type the Email -> Click Send.
3. Create conversions for actions that you would like to track on your site.

4. Create or update your Ad to track conversions from your site.
5. Get Pixel Helper to check that your pixel is working.
6. View reporting and results from the pixel.
7. Adjust your ad or campaign accordingly.

To install the pixel on your website (Step 2) you'll need to paste the JavaScript code snippet between **<head>** and **</head>** on every page of your site. If you're using Wordpress, we recommend the Header and Footer plugin to allow you to do this simply.

If your business has an app, you can also create a custom audience to reach people who take specific actions in your app — like reaching a specific level in a game, adding items to their cart or rating your app. Start measuring events in your app by integrating Facebook's SDK for iOS, Android, and Canvas. Every time someone takes the specified action within your app, they will be added to your Custom Audience.

After you've created your custom audience, you can take it one step further and create Lookalike Audiences with the Custom Audiences that you have already created. Facebook looks at all the characteristic of the customers that you have provided in your custom audience, and finds other people who share these characteristics. Lookalike Audiences are perfect for fan acquisition, website registration, brand awareness and off-Facebook purchases as it opens up your brand to a new group of people who, whilst they might be unfamiliar to you now, have some significant shared traits with your target audience.

Please Note: Your Lookalike Audience can only include people from one country at a time, and there needs to be more than 100 people from that country present in your Custom Audience.

When creating a Lookalike Audience, choose your Source, Country and your Audience Size. Although the Audience Size can range from 1% to 10% of your target country, it is always best to stick with relatively low numbers so that you're only picking the most targeted audience members. As a general guide, most businesses find they get the best response with a lookalike audience below 5%.

Let's break this down with an exercise covering what we've learned:

The Cirque du Ninja is creating a spectacular new fire-breathing acrobatics show in Toronto, Ontario. They have all the choreography created, but there is one thing missing: performers. They've put out numerous ads in the paper for performers with no luck and they are at their wit's end!

How might you create an ad to help with their recruitment?

1. You've clicked "create ad" and are faced with 9 options: Boost Post, Promote Page, Send people to your Website. Which option would work best in this type of situation?

    1. Boost post
    2. Promote page
    3. Send People to your website
    4. Increase conversions on your website

Let's quickly run down the list and find the best possible option. A boosted post could be an option. You would have a clickable box that would send individuals to the registration page and you could use a picture that shows the sort of performers you're after. But there is one thing missing from a boosted post: a call to action. Individuals tend to respond better with a call to action, such as "Sign up", "Buy now", "Enter here" etc. Plus a boosted post does not give you the option of tracking conversions with a Facebook Pixel. So even though it could work, it's not the best option.

Second, Promote your Page. Irrelevant here as we aren't promoting the page (although you could create a "Circus Jobs in Ontario" page and promote that!).

'Send people to your website' could work, as it'd get people onto the site where you could pixel them to create Custom and LookaLike audiences for future casting campaigns.

But the most suitable option here is 'Increase website conversions to your website'. This option is specifically made to send people to your website to take a specific action, like signing up for casting. Of all the options mostly likely to work, this is the most suitable any time you have a specific conversion goal in mind.

You'll need to set up your Facebook Pixel, put it on every page of your website, and tweak the code on the sign up 'thank you' page so that Facebook recognises visits to that page as a conversion.

You'll now be prompted to choose your conversion type: View Content, Purchase, Register, or Add To Cart.

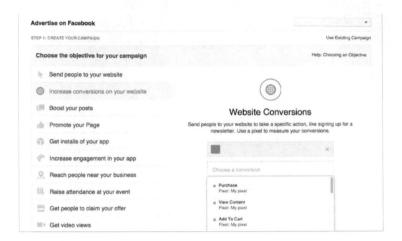

Once you've chosen 'Register', it's time to target your ad. How would you target if you were looking for the sort of female dancers who'd be open to appearing in Cirque de Ninja?

First, location. Targeting Toronto, Ontario and its radius is too specific of an audience for our ads to be shown because this is the sort of role that our audience would be willing to travel for, so let's make it broader. You might decide to target provinces, cities and states around Toronto, for example: New York, Pennsylvania and Ohio. Next, Gender: Female. Language: your prerogative (but let's just pick English, as the ad will probably be in English).

166

At this stage you can choose to create two different types of ads. You can focus your campaign on people that have used the word "dance" in their job title like "Dancer", "Dance Teacher" and "Dance artist". Or if you want to go broader, you can target people who have expressed an interest in dance through liking pages and visiting websites relating to dance.

To make sure that you are targeting the right people, Facebook shows a dial indicating how well your audience is targeted" Red (audience too specific), Amber (audience too broad), Green (just right). A highly targeted audience is ideal as it produces higher CTRs (click-through rates), due to greater relevancy. In the end, it is all about identifying your niche, because niche audiences, while tiny in comparison to broad campaigns, have built-in conversion intent (whether it is purchasing intent or something else like registering for castings!) Once you finish targeting, establish a budget, and make sure to create a captivating ad by creating a call-to-action button.

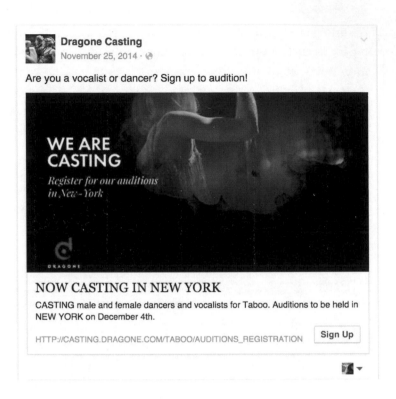

Your Landing Page

A final important consideration when advertising on Facebook is the page that you are sending people to in your ad. Conversion rates vary, but a very general ballpark guide is that your landing page should be converting around 1% of the visitors your ads are serving. If you're getting more than this, great. If not, there are only two possible explanations.

Firstly, it could be that your ads aren't targeted enough. You might want to try narrowing your audience to show ads only to those most likely to convert, or try a Custom Audience of your existing fans or customers to check that your offering is attractive.

The second possibility is that something about the page people are landing on is turning them off. If you suspect that this is the case, check Google Analytics to see what your bounce rate is (the percentage of people that leave the site without visiting any other pages), and try the page on different devices to make sure that the mobile experience in particular is up to scratch.

Common causes of bounce rate from landing pages can include:

- Imagery very different to that used in the ad. To prevent people from feeling unfamiliar with the landing page, it's a good idea to keep the images similar (or identical) to those used in the ad. They clicked on the ad, after all, so it makes sense that they like the look of the image or product it promotes.
- Slow page loading times. Particularly on mobile, your audience is far less forgiving than you might hope when it comes to the speed that your website loads. Radware found that 51% of net users cited site speed as the top reason they'd abandon a purchase.

- Lack of focus in the message. Your landing page is there to do one thing, and one thing only. Don't try to sell your products or services if you want someone to fill in a form - sell the form to them. Don't distract them from the thing you brought them to the site to do.

- Lack of trust signals. If you're driving people to a product page from your ad, does that page give the visitor enough information about the product to *really* make the purchase? We get sent a lot of under-performing e-commerce websites to review, and typically we'll hit a product page to see one sentence of generic copy and 2 generic pictures. Is that enough for someone to buy a product from a website they've never heard of? Look at the *work* Amazon does to convert visitors: lengthy descriptions, product images, videos, dozens/hundreds/thousands of reviews, manufacturer information... and that's to convert visitors who already know about Amazon, and have shopped from there multiple times in the past.

Facebook Summary

Whether through a Business Page, Ads, or both, Facebook undoubtedly gives businesses the largest marketing platform of any of the social channels. The difference between an amateur and Ninja Facebook campaign is as much about the time spent familiarising yourself with the page audience and making sure that the content is well-targeted, high engagement and actually *interesting*, as it is about having a huge audience. The businesses that do best from Facebook aren't always the ones with millions of likes - they're they ones who understand their audience so well that each post and ad elicits the maximum response.

So commit to making your Facebook page the most useful, interesting or entertaining page your audience engages with, and you can't go too far wrong.

Twitter

Most businesses doing really well with social either find Facebook or Twitter to be the network that delivers the best results for them.

In a similar way to Facebook, the most effective Twitter profiles have a definite 'persona' and, where possible, they engage with their audience on a 1:1 basis as often as possible.

Twitter encourages more interaction than Facebook, so you might find that a one-dimensional 'broadcast' approach doesn't cut it. Just like a conversation you have with a group of friends, people get a little annoyed if you constantly keep talking about yourself. Yes, your audience wants to see your content, but (depending on the brand) they also want to see that you are interested in your community. Innocent Drinks (@innocent) does this particularly well, often responding to fan Tweets and Retweeting them to strengthen their own messages, but also show that they engage and encourage their followers to Tweet them.

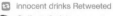
Call me Lalaa @AngelaNakiyingi · Nov 15
First time tasting @innocent new coconut water. So tasty and
refreshing

↩   ⇄ 1   ♥ 10   •••

Profitable Twitter Marketing

So what makes the difference between the millions of
empty, low-engagement Twitter accounts and the
businesses that use this tool to generate traffic, sales
and familiarity?

Just like any marketing channel, a Ninja Twitter
campaign will follow the 3Ms: right **message**, right
market and right **media**. The sort of **message** that
tends to work best on Twitter is slightly different to the
approach that works best on Facebook. Of course on
Twitter we have the 140 character limit on each Tweet,
but we also have @replies and #hashtags at our
disposal and both can be useful to get your Tweets
some extra visibility.

Eighty percent of Twitter's 300 million active users use it on their mobiles, and the average Twitter user spends almost three hours per month on it according to Hubspot. It's the content of their Tweets that gives us the biggest indication of why Twitter is so different to Facebook though: 68% of all Tweets are replies to other Tweets. It's this interaction, combined with the fast decay of Tweets (unlike Facebook, Tweets are strictly ordered by age, so old Tweets are essentially invisible) that exemplifies the Twitter difference. News and events break fast on Twitter — much faster than Facebook — and the instantaneous visibility of Tweets means that those who Tweet regularly are rewarded with greater exposure.

The Super Bowl, the Grammys and SNL 40th Anniversary special were the most Tweeted about events in 2014-2015. These are all short events that people participate in conversations about, *live*. On Facebook, by contrast, the most popular topics in 2014 were things such as the Ebola outbreak, the World Cup and the Ice Bucket Challenge. These events tend to play out over a longer period of time and generate a longer 'tail'. Visit Twitter three hours after an event, and there's very little sign of any mentions; the conversation has largely moved on and the new Tweets have 'covered' the topic. On Facebook however, you'll still see the most engaging posts from the day and the conversation is still very visible.

So what sort of content works best on Twitter? The sort of content that works well on *all* social networks: a mixture of entertainment, information and the occasional appropriate pitch. Let's dissect some accounts that get fantastic engagement, and see what sort of strategy they use to do it.

Case Study 1: Fast Company (@FastCompany)

Technology and business magazine Fast Company's goal is website traffic, which they can monetise through adverts and by selling magazine subscriptions. Their Twitter feed is almost exclusively their own content, and their Tweets have a very set formula:

94 Fast Company @FastCompany · 2h
Driverless, electric taxis could reduce
emissions by 94%: f-st.co/83GIULJ

↩   ↱ 54   ♥ 35   •••

 94 Fast Company @FastCompany · 3h
10 graphic design visionairies you should
know: f-st.co/22jSwgT

↩   ↱ 43   ♥ 63   •••

Descriptive headline, link to the blog post and then an image. The use of the images breaks up their feed and gives a quick clue to the content of the article. They also follow a pretty strict two Tweets per hour schedule, which keeps them visible in their followers' feeds.

Case Study 2: Vala Afshar (@ValaAfshar)

Salesforce Chief Digital Evangelist, Vala's Twitter feed is an example of a perfect 'personal brand' approach to Twitter. His 4-6 Tweets an hour are mostly interesting facts, statistics about technology and widely used principles:

Vala Afshar @ValaAfshar · 18h
How people ignored each other before smartphones

↩   ⟲ 252   ♥ 183   •••

His Tweet frequency can be *very* high - usually up to six Tweets per hour, but sometimes as many as 10. What is most interesting about Vala is that his Tweets don't seem to be particularly focused on building an audience of Salesforce prospects; he seems to be building his own personal brand as an interesting person.

You'll probably have noticed some commonalities between the case studies above and the Twitter accounts you most closely follow, so let's look at the general principles of a successful profile.

The Do's and Don'ts of Twitter

- **DO be visual:** people want to see Tweets with images, GIFs, and/or videos attached to them. As soon as Twitter started embedding images in its feed, it moved from being a purely text medium to being one of the most visual. The

178

sort of content that works well is striking, self-explanatory or designed to arouse curiosity (if the goal is to elicit a click).

- **DON'T rely too heavily on automation bots:** Many companies and individuals use annoying auto-messaging software to thank new followers, post out their stats from the week or a range of other pointless topics. At best, it waters down your feed and makes you look spammy. At worst, things can turn sticky: Bank of America experienced the wrath of angry Twitter users recently when it misguidedly tried to diffuse the complaints of an angry dad who'd had his house foreclosed. When other Tweeters joined in calling out the bank and displaying their anger at the repossessions, the bank started sending out generic messages: "We'd be happy to review your account with you to address any concerns. Please let us know if you need assistance". This didn't really help the situation, which quickly got out of hand. The bank later explained that actually the Tweets came from live responders, but by then the damage was done.

- **DO have a strategy to communicate with you audience:** Just like any social media the voice and tone that your brand will use on Twitter when answering positive and negative feedback defines the personality that people associate with you. When @amberkarnes

179

accused Urban Outfitters of stealing designs for their clothing, the 'Twitterverse' jumped on the story. Urban Outfitters clearly had no strategy to respond in this type of situation, issuing a half-baked attempt to clear up the mess. It was nowhere near enough though and the brand lost 17,000 followers. Both #urbanoutfitters and #thieves were trending in just a few hours.

Meanwhile @argos turned a complaint about low stock levels and employees with attitude into a viral customer service smash:

Immy 'BADMAN' Bugti
@BadManBugti
8 Mar 14

@Argos_Online YO wen u gettin da ps4 tings in moss side? Ain't waitin no more. Plus da asian guy whu works dere got bare attitude #wasteman

Argos Helpers ✓
@ArgosHelpers

Follow

@BadManBugti Safe badman, we gettin sum more PS4 tings in wivin da next week y'get me. Soz bout da attitude, probz avin a bad day yo.

LD
8:26 AM - 8 Mar 2014
↩ ⟲ 9,096 ♥ 5,384

Immy 'BADMAN' Bugti
@BadManBugti

Follow

@ArgosHelpers respect. Sick guy
8:31 AM - 8 Mar 2014
↩ ⟲ 351 ♥ 293

- **DON'T be an egoist:** Twitter is a community and sharing other people's Tweets and information is a good way to start a conversation. With the exception of pure content publishers (Fast Company in the previous example), people *expect* businesses to share, and it should not be considered weakness to curate content from elsewhere.

- **DO share exclusive access:** Give your Twitter followers special promotions or exclusive information that others 'on the outside' don't get access to. This feeling of exclusivity is a good way to keep people coming back for more.
- **DON'T be insensitive**: Trying to make money by taking advantage of sad events is considered opportunistic and generally doesn't go down too well on Twitter! @Tweetbox360 Tweeted "Remember Amy Winehouse by downloading the ground-breaking 'Back to Back' over at Zune" It's a fine line between taking advantage of opportunities to sell more and being insensitive and the Twittersphere didn't take kindly to the former.
- **DO keep it short:** Tweets with less than 50 characters tend to drive the highest engagement so make sure to keep your Tweet under 100 characters if you plan on including a link and photo. Multi-Tweet messages are generally a no-no, as they get split up in people's feeds. If you have a longer message to share, post a photo of it or write a compelling headline and direct people to a longer-form blog post instead.
- **DO Tweet frequently:** Due to the immediacy and much faster decay of Tweets compared to Facebook posts, your audience will generally put up with a much higher post frequency. If your audience spans the globe you'll need to

182

bear in mind the times of day each country is most likely to be using Twitter so you can time your Tweets accordingly. It's also acceptable to repost the same Tweet during the day in order to boost its visibility for each time zone, although clearly this can be overdone as well!

- **DON'T follow everyone, DO follow specific people:** Many brands and individuals maintain a habit of following back people who follow them. You can use this to grow your follower base by following others in your industry hoping that when they see the notification of your follow, they'll decide to follow back. It's worth remembering that they'll see your tagline when deciding whether or not to follow you, so of course it's extremely important that your tagline reflects not only who you are and what you do, but indicates a benefit for those who will be following you: "follow for the latest developments in medical recruiting", for example. However just following everyone you can find skews your Follows/Follower ratio, which alters people's perception of your Twitter page. The most authoritative profiles have many more followers than they follow, so always be mindful of this ratio, and consider using an app like JustUnfollow to remove those who don't interest you or that haven't followed you back.

- **DO use strategic URL's:** according to SocialBro 2014 Data, "Tweets from businesses with a URL placed in the middle of the a Tweet are 26% more likely to get Retweeted than Tweets with the URL placed at the beginning or end of the Tweet." Remember always to 'sell' any link you post with a compelling and descriptive headline and, where possible, a picture.
- **DO use a use a link shortener:** Bit.ly, Ow.ly and/or Goo.gl can make the Tweet look clean and less cluttered, giving you more space for an interesting message! These services can also give you analytics data, to show you how many people clicked your link, and when.

The Perfect Hashtags

Hashtags are incredibly important on Twitter as they allow people to join conversations about things that interest them. As brands, we can also jump in on these conversations, provided that we obey the basic hashtag etiquette.

For those unfamiliar with the Hashtag process, including a word with a has (#) at the start makes it a clickable hashtag on Twitter. By clicking on the Hashtag, it's possible to see all the other Tweets that use that Hashtag. For example, when a popular TV show like The Apprentice is live, thousands of people will take to Twitter and Tweet their opinions about what's happening, using the Hashtag #theapprentice or #apprentice. Others watching will search for mentions of this Hashtag to see what people are saying.

Let's dig a little bit deeper and look at different types of hashtags out here:

User-generated: These are ad hoc hashtags that have been naturally and organically adopted by Twitter users. For example #Londontravel or #IloveLondon. They receive occasional use, and aren't focused around a particular event.

Events: Almost every major event has a hashtag, from the #Oscars2016 to #LFW (London Fashion Week). Exhibitors and brands involved with events can piggyback off these hashtags to gain more exposure amongst attendees and those at home keeping up with the event on Twitter.

Always-on: There are certain hashtags that have their own niches and communities around them, like #ttot ("travel talk on Twitter", used by travel bloggers) or #ThrowbackThursday (a celebration of the past, every Thursday. People use this Hashtag and post images, Tweets or content 'throwbacks'). These sort of evergreen hashtags can be used to tap into a specific audience or just generally demonstrate awareness of Twitter communities.

Branded: Sometimes a brand will create their own Hashtag to tie in with an ad campaign or link

185

themselves to an event. For example, a client of ours was running a Halloween promotion, so we created the Hashtag #PkScream to tie their Halloween posts together.

Unbranded: Tweets that are still unique but do not feature the brand name in it, such as the Charmin #Tweetfromtheseat campaign. The campaign is still unique to Charmin but instead of focusing on the brand name, the focus is around the concept.

In short, #hashtags should be:

- Short and sweet. If it isn't short, then make sure it's catchy. Charmin and its #Tweetfromtheseat are a perfect example of how to make a longer hashtag work.
- Broad enough to get traffic, and yet specific enough to be targeted. Are you writing about travel in London? Ditch the #London hashtag and replace it with something like #Londontravel
- Seamlessly integrated into your Tweet, when possible: "Did you know that #Panamahats are actually made in Ecuador? Snagged this handmade one at #WTM15."
- Piggyback off event hashtags like the one we used above. #WTM15 stands for the World Travel Market 2015 that was held in London in November 2015. Using this sort of event hashtag can give you serious exposure to the

186

visitors of that event if the timing and topic is optimal.

- Unique, if you want to measure spread. If you're running a large campaign, you might want to create your own unique hashtag so that you can easily search for mentions, comments and the reach/impressions of the campaign on Twitter. Decide whether a branded or unbranded hashtag would work better for your campaign.
- Limited to one or two per Tweet. Too many Hashtags, and you risk #Hashtagblindness. #Dontgothere #stayclassy. #thatsenough.

Live Tweeting & Twitter Chats

'Live Tweeting' events, TV shows and conferences that your audience is already engaging with is like joining their conversation at a party. It gives you a chance to communicate your brand's opinion and get on people's radars.

For B2B Tweeters, Tweeting statistics and useful nuggets from conference talks using the conference hashtag can allow those who are following at home or who are in different talks to keep up with the conversation. At every conference there is usually a handful of hardcore live Tweeters who Tweet every talk they're in - some as much as multiple times per minute. Providing that their Tweets are useful, they'll usually be able to pick up as many as 25-100 new followers per hour just by being extremely visible - even if they add none of their own personality or opinions.

The secret to maximising the effects of your live Tweeting is to give the Tweets as much context as possible and make sure they work as useful 'standalone' snippets. Your goal is to give such useful snippets that your audience Retweets them, for example:

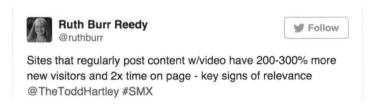

Ruth Burr Reedy
@ruthburr

Follow

Sites that regularly post content w/video have 200-300% more new visitors and 2x time on page - key signs of relevance @TheToddHartley #SMX

That statistic is definitely a 'Tweetable', and Ruth has included the Twitter handle of the speaker too, which is good conference etiquette and increases the likelihood of that person responding or thanking her for the Tweet after their talk.

If you're live Tweeting and you see something interesting, snap a photo of it and add this to your Tweet. Tweets that include a picture get 150% more Retweets, so whether you're snapping an interesting conference slide or picture from a TV show, as long as you give context in the text of your Tweet, you should find it gives you a nice bump.

Part of the benefit of Live Tweeting is the relationships that you can build through the shared experience. Run a search for the hashtag on Twitter and keep checking back for new Tweets, particularly those from people that are especially active. Live tweeters who are getting a lot of Retweets and interactions might be expressing widely shared views or could have a lot of authority on this topic. They might make good contacts. Those who are asking lots of questions might be the ones Live Tweeting for the feeling of involvement and community, and are more likely to respond back if you reach out to them. If you see questions that you can answer, do so. If you see insightful Tweets from others, Retweet them. If you find people that could be useful contacts or customers, follow them — they'll be checking you out when they see the follow notification.

Before we move on let's look at a really *good* example of live event hashtags, and an example of a business that totally bailed on a popular hashtag that went out of control.

First the good example:

@Wordstream (who provide marketing software) wrote a post with their favourite statistics from a bunch of conferences attended by their target audience. This was genius because everyone loves stats, and the post was Tweeted 115 times in three days. But it's their use of the conference hashtags that takes this Tweet to the Hall of Fame, because it gets them on the radar of attendees for each of these conferences. Then they slapped an attention-grabbing image on, and made it into this book. Ninjas.

An example of a live Tweeting opportunity that went awry comes courtesy of London lettings agency @CapitalLiving. Excited to be featured on a TV documentary, in the run up to the show they continually posted Tweets encouraging their followers to tune in. As soon as 'How To Live The Chelsea Life' started however, it became apparent that this was not going to be a good night for the agency. Their open practice of excluding those tenants that didn't fit a very tight set of predefined criteria riled many of the watchers, as did the owner's treatment of a tradesman. Viewers headed straight to Twitter to voice their opinions. The hashtag #capitalliving began trending and the verdict was unanimous. @WhatLauraLoves wasn't feeling the love:

 **WhatLauraLoves**
@whatlauraloves   ✿   +☺ Follow

Watching this #HowToLiveTheChelseaLife programme with #CapitalLiving ... Adam is absolutely awful. Showing his company to be elitist racist!

@katieTweets26 wrote:

How did @capitalliving respond to this barrage? By making their Facebook and Twitter pages private. Rather than respond, issue any sort of apology or retraction, they opted for radio silence and people continued bashing them in their absence.

Twitter Chats

Twitter chats (or Tweetchats) are similar to live Tweeting in the sense that they're an online discussion around a specific topic, such as travel or technology, although they're not linked to an outside event. Companies and blogs run Tweetchats to discuss a particular topic with their audience, or invite a celebrity to host a Q&A from their feed.

Each chat has a specific theme and an accompanying Hashtag, either unique or established. For example, #travelchat is an established Twitter chat Hashtag about travel, but in the example above you can see that A Travelling Broad has focussed the topic more narrowly in order to give the chat some structure. Themes under #travelchat could be solo travel, travel safety, beach travel and so on. Chats usually typically last an hour, and sometimes the leader of the chat will post new questions every ten minutes in a format of Q1, Q2, Q3. Tweeters participating in the chat will often start their Tweets with A1, A2, A3, and include the chat Hashtag so as to be seen by the organiser and other participants.

Sometimes a brand will sponsor a chat in order to be mentioned by the host, who might also decide to revolve the chat around a product that the brand has to offer.

A great example is the #TripItChat hosted every month by travel superstars @ThePlanetD and sponsored by @TripItm, a trip planner/itinerary application. In this particular example, the brand (@TripItm) decided to partner with an influencer (@ThePlanetD) and create a branded hashtag that includes the name of the company: #TripItChat. TripIt also join in during each chat, commenting on answers and Retweeting interesting ones. Why does it work? PlanetD (which has over 114K followers on Twitter) starts a conversation on wanderlust, talking about far-away destinations and sharing some epic travel photos, using this branded Hashtag. The response they get from their highly engaged audience is huge, with many Tweeting back, also using this branded Hashtag. Through the sponsorship they are introducing their audience to a company that 1) they probably have never heard of (new audience) and 2) can help them achieve their wanderlust (relevance). For TripIt, this is a highly effective and non sales-y way to generate some positive associations with a highly relevant audience.

Growing Your Following

Let's talk about some ways to increase your Twitter following, starting with picking up follows from those you're already in contact with.

Engaging With Current Contacts

If growing your social presence is important, you might consider including a link to your Twitter page in company-wide email signatures. To increase the chances of someone taking action and clicking the link, you can include a Call To Action: "Follow us on Twitter to get exclusive Twitter-only offers, real-time service updates and see behind the scenes at our HQ!"

You can also build Twitter interaction into your CRM. By asking for customers' Twitter handles when they make the purchase, you can Tweet them that their order has been received or their product has been dispatched. The novelty of our order status being Tweeted to them is just too much to resist for many, and you'll find that they can't help but Retweet you along with a comment about how excited they are. BH Cosmetics (@bhcosmetics) frequently Tweet their customers about order status, and as a result their Twitter @replies are mostly customer service interactions. It doesn't work for everyone though; adult toys and male enhancement stores should probably give this strategy a miss.

Twitter's Find Friends service means you can give Twitter access to your email account and have it crawl your contacts for people who have Twitter profiles. You can then choose to follow them, and, depending on the depth of your relationship, you'll pick up some reciprocal follows from this.

How To Get Retweeted More Often

One of the best ways to get new followers is to be Retweeted, particularly by those who have an audience relevant to your message.

A Cornell study analysed 1.7 million Tweets in order to identify the characteristics of those that were Retweeted (shared) most often and found that:

- It helps to ask people to share. Calls to Action on Twitter work. According to Hubspot, "Please Retweet" is the 11th most Retweeted phrase, so it does drive Retweets, even if it can risk looking a bit desperate when overused.
- Being informative helps. People Retweet useful or interesting things, so that their audience can get the same benefit. This makes the Retweeter look good in the eyes of their followers, which is exactly how you want them to feel when they share your content.
- Sounding like your community boosts authenticity. Every community has their own language, whether it's car body shops talking about PDR (Paintless Glue Removal) or Startups talking about Series A (investment). By using the buzzwords and insider language, you give your audience that sense of being a part of something that is *such* a motivator for social media usage.
- Imitating headlines boosts engagement. The Buzzfeed style of headline sounds hype-y, but really works. "A Chart About Silence That Will Leave You Speechless" and "This Woman's Massive Instagram Following Helped Her Launch a Business" are way more engaging than "How men and women voted in the 2012

election" and "How Laura Kasperzak uses Instagram", which are equally as descriptive of the content in those articles. Buzzfeed even built a Random Headline Generator (http://www.buzzfeed.com/scott/the-buzzfeed-headline-generator#.shgJ03P601) to help you practice with the style.

- Generality helps ("a" and "an" rather than "the").
- The easier to read, the better. The average length of a viral headline is 62 characters, so make it short and sharp.

Using the data from their study, the Cornell team built a tool that can predict the likelihood of a Tweet being Retweeted, based on the language used: https://chenhaot.com/Retweetedmore/

Scheduling Your Tweets

Because of the almost instant decay in the visibility of your Tweets, the days and times that you post are crucial. A study by Buffer found that early mornings are generally the best time to Tweet if you want to attract *clicks*, whilst *favourites* and *Retweets* are most common late in the evening and at night. Despite this, most Tweets are posted around lunchtime: between noon and 1pm.

Of course all of this comes with a comprehensive list of caveats:

1. The best time for you to Tweet will depend on your audience's time zone. If your audience spans multiple time zones, you might want to duplicate your Tweets to arrive at the right time for each audience. Tools like Followerwonk (https://moz.com/followerwonk/) can help you spot when your audience is online.
2. The times that your audience is most active obviously depends on their lifestyle and schedule. Office workers have a very different day to mummy bloggers, for example. Ideally you want to be posting whilst your audience is in no-pressure work mode. In other words they're *thinking* about work, but not necessarily *doing* work.
3. Just to throw another spanner in the works, posting at the busiest time of day might not even be the best option for your business, as the competition for eyeballs is so much higher. If you Tweet during quiet periods, your Tweets will have a longer life on the timeline and could attract more engagement as a result.

The takeaway from all of this is to start a schedule based on the best educated guess you can make, and refine it over time as you get feedback from your audience and begin to notice engagement trends. We use Buffer to help with scheduling as it gives analysis on the times that have brought your best engagement historically, and then allows you to automatically schedule your Tweets to be posted at these times. You can select the frequency of your Tweets (once, twice, one hundred times per day), and any Tweets you drop into Buffer's queue will be saved to automatically post at those times.

Hootsuite (https://hootsuite.com) is a very popular social media management platform and has a free plan that also allows you to schedule your Tweets, although it doesn't give you the automatic scheduling options that Buffer does. We'll look at social management tools in more depth later on.

Twitter Ads

BY THE NUMBERS

302M | **1B** | **500M** | **80%**

Monthly Active Users | Tweets sent every two days | Unique logged-out users every month | of active users are mobile

Source | Twitter internal Data (August 2013-April 2015)

Twitter Ads give you the opportunity to get your Tweets more visibility than they'd ordinarily get in amongst the 5,800 Tweets pumped into the Twittersphere every single second.

It's important to say that Twitter's Ad platform is relatively basic when compared to Facebook, and the targeting is nowhere near as precise. This is largely unavoidable because we tell Twitter far less about

199

ourselves than we do Facebook, but that's not to say the platform can't be a useful in our arsenal. There are three different types of promoted products:

Promote Account: This gives your Twitter profile a top spot in the 'who to follow' section, or puts you directly in your target audience's timeline with an embedded 'follow' button. The purpose of Promoted Account campaigns is to grow your follower numbers.

Promoted Tweet: This gives one of your regular Tweets extra visibility to an audience that can be finely targeted. Promoted Tweets extend the reach and frequency of your Tweets by placing them at the top of relevant search results or within user timelines when they ordinarily would have been 'covered up' by more recent Tweets.

Promoted Trend: Trending topics are the most active conversations that are happening on Twitter at any moment. A promoted trend allows your brand to rise to the top of this topic list for a 24-hour period.

With Promoted Accounts you pay each time someone follows your account. Promoted Tweets are charged each time someone Retweets or engages with that Tweet. Once the ad is finished, Twitter gives you insights from the campaign, including the number of impressions, engagements, the amount you spent and the conversions the campaign achieved. It also allows for an in-depth analysis giving you the ability to look at the platforms that were most popular, the locations that your Ad was seen, and demographics of those who engaged. Just as with Facebook ads, these insights are key because they allow better targeting of future ads, resulting in more cost-effective campaigns.

Across the top of your Twitter Ads analytics dashboard, you'll find different tabs for impressions (the number of times your ad was seen), engagements (clicks, follows, Retweets etc.), and ad spend per day and conversions.

Similar to Facebook ads, for each Twitter ad you run you'll set a goal; you might be driving clicks to your website, follows of your profile or conversions (conversion tracking involves placing a piece of Twitter code on your thank you page). The number of times this goal is achieved is shown in the Results column. The conversion rate (3) is the number of conversions divided by the number of times your ad was seen, and the Cost per Result (4) is the amount spent to bring each Result.

The targeting options you have for your Twitter ads are:

202

Geography: Here you can choose the target geography that you want your Tweets to be visible in. Note that if you target a specific zip/postal code, your Tweets will show to people *currently in* that zip code, not necessarily those that *live* in that zip code. This is perfect for local stores that want to appear on the radars of people visiting the area, and the limited reach keeps costs relatively low.

Gender: No prizes for guessing this one!

Language: This allows you to target users that Twitter has deemed understand a particular language. If you want to target Polish speaking Brits you can target those located in the UK but who understand Polish. If they've Tweeted in Polish or set their profile language to Polish, your ad should reach them.

Device Targeting: specific by OS version, device or WIFI connectivity. Perfect for those targeting App installs, webinars or flash-based websites which would all likely require different landing pages/App Store links for each type of device.

Followers: If your target audience can't get enough of a particular authority figure, get in front of them all in one go by piggybacking this person's authority and targeting their followers. You can also target users that are *similar* to this person's followers - perfect if they have a very relevant audience, but you'd like to go a bit wider.

Interest Targeting: Target people based on the interests they talk about and engage with on Twitter. Interests are broken down by category (e.g.

Automotive, Business, Careers) and subcategories (e.g. within business: Entrepreneurship, Leadership, Investments).

Keywords: Here you can target people that have searched, Tweeted about or engaged with specific keywords.

Television: Reach people who engage with specific TV programming, such as particular shows, genres or TV networks.

Tailored Audiences: Similar to Custom Audiences on Facebook, Tailored Audiences allows you to reach people who have shown interest in your brand outside of Twitter. This means you can use your own emails lists, site visitors or a list of Twitter IDs to segment and target relevant audiences for your campaign.

If you've noticed larger ads in your feed that invite you to sign up, watch buy a product or download an app, you've seen Twitter Cards in action. These more advanced ads usually come with a photo and a call to action (CTA) button. There are four types of twitter cards that you can create:

Website Card: feature your website content and have a call to action button (usually visit now), driving people directly to your website.

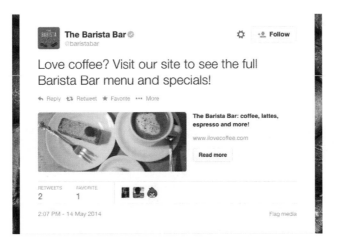

Lead Generation Card: Offer your audience the chance to sign up for your mailing list just by clicking a button. When they do this, Twitter will give you the email address they've registered for Twitter with. You can take this a step further and create a custom landing page that directs people away from Twitter so that you can collect more data.

Promote Video: One-click play function that includes an interactive CTA.

Mobile App Card: Showcase you app and direct people to download it in the Google/App Store. Note that your app needs a super clear value proposition and will usually need to be free for this CTA to be the most effective option.

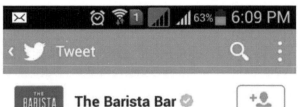

Even if you never pay a penny to Twitter Ads, the analytics that it gives you is useful to understand the sort of Tweets that get best engagement from your audience, and to see how your audience is growing.

Visit https://ads.twitter.com/, login and choose Analytics from the menu.

Your Account home screen gives you a useful overview of your performance over the each month, including your top Tweets, highest profile new followers, the number of followers acquired and monthly engagements.

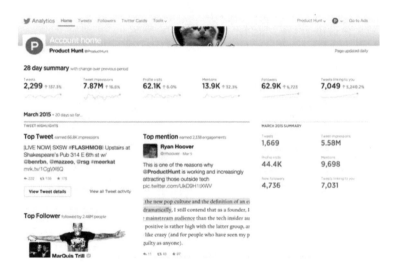

You can click an individual Tweet to see its activity:

If you want to delve even deeper, Audience insights shows you information about your followers based on their interests, language, lifestyle type, buying style, mobile footprint, household income and more. Just like Facebook Insights, Twitter's Insights highlight trends in the demographics and interests of your audience so that you can target your Tweets to get more engagement from this audience.

Twitter Summary

Twitter's main USPs is the conversation elements (encompassing Hashtags, trending topics and @replies) and the speed. Whilst these give us plenty to play with, they also mean that growing a Twitter profile can require a lot of effort. Keeping Tweet frequency up, monitoring trends, finding influencers and live Tweeting all take time and generally it's not as easy to shortcut audience growth through Ads as it is on Facebook.

Like Facebook, Twitter is an essential element of any business or brand's profitable social media campaign. The outreach opportunities are unparalleled, offering fast access to any almost influencer in any market. For that alone, Twitter *has* to be a priority.

Instagram

With more than 300 million monthly active users, Instagram is the most popular image-based social network. Since it was launched at the end of 2010, over 30 billion photos and videos have been published. On average, 70 million pieces of content are posted each and every day, according to data from Instagram blog.

The widely held perception is that Instagram is mostly used by young people with a skew to those who are well educated and have disposable income. These generalisations seem to be supported by the data: according to the *Instagram 2015 Study* carried out by Iconosquare, the 15-35 year old age bracket is over-represented on Instagram with a 73% share, while the 35-50 bracket represents 14% of users. The study found that most of these instagrammers either work (48%) or are student (43%). They also generally have a higher education degree (46%) including 12% with postgraduate degrees.

Generally, the presence of brands on Instagram is well received provided they are sensitive to what users are on Instagram for in the first place (beautiful images). Unsurprisingly then fashion, beauty and decoration are incredibly popular, whilst finance, software and businesses selling commoditised or un-extraordinary products tend to be less so.

An Instagram account gives a business a chance to present its trendiest and most visually appealing face, and allows access to this young and up-to-date audience. To a greater extent than Facebook and Twitter then, the content of your Instagram page needs to be tailored to fit with the sort of content that does well on Instagram. Posting endless uninspiring product photos or unappealing pictures of your business premises or logo won't work here, as Instagrammers just won't follow profiles that post unattractive pictures.

Laura Ashley's Instagram feed (https://www.instagram.com/lauraashleyuk) for example, isn't stuffed full of promotional and commercial messages. It's almost entirely beautiful shots of their products in context, with the occasionally targeted offer, whether that's promoting the launch of a new collection or running a contest to drive engagement. Even the McDonald's account has gorgeous photos: https://www.instagram.com/mcdonalds/.

To turn up on Instagram and start posting unattractive images is like turning up at a sports bar wearing the opposition's kit.

Setting Up An Instagram Account

Instagram is a mobile app that you can download on iOS and Android phones and tablets as well as Windows Phone 8 and later. You **must** create your account using the Instagram mobile app, not a computer. After you've downloaded the app and created an account you'll be able to see your Instagram posts from a computer, but it's definitely a mobile-first network.

Linking on Instagram

Unlike Facebook and Twitter, you can't post links in your Instagram posts. The only clickable link Instagram allows you is on your profile page, in the 'About Me' section.

This obviously poses challenges if your primary social media goal is to generate traffic to your website. What we've found to be most successful here is to offer some appealing 'bait' in your profile section, and link to a landing page on your website where visitors can submit their details to download this bait.

You'll notice Instagrammers saying things like "To grab your free gift with every order this weekend click the link in our profile and use voucher code INSTA123". There is also nothing to stop you from changing this single link during different promotions and offers to drive people to different products or landing pages, although you'll want to make sure to leave each link up long enough that you don't have recent posts referring to a link that no longer exists.

Really? I've GOT to use my phone?

If the thought of being tied to your mobile to create Instagram images is too much, there are workarounds that allow you to do the work on your computer and still post through your phone. Although there are apps that allow desktop uploads to Instagram (none of which are particularly mention-worthy), the best method is to use Dropbox synced on your desktop and your mobile phone.

The method is quite simple:

- Download Dropbox on your computer and get the mobile app for iPhone/Android.
- On your desktop, create or edit the pictures you need.
- Save these to Dropbox.
- On your mobile, open the Dropbox app and save your photos (which will be sync'd from your desktop) to your camera roll or as a separate album on the phone.
- Upload to Instagram from your phone.

Simple!

Hashtags

As on Twitter, Instagram Hashtags allow you to find new audiences for your photos and grow your following. The same basic rules apply to Hashtags on any network, in that you want to choose tags that have sufficient popularity, are targeted enough to your images/products and are actually relevant to what you're posting.

With no limit to caption length, you're free to write longer posts and include more Hashtags. In the above example you can see how @JamieOliver has given some explanation for what's in the picture and used the #breakfast and #brunch tags to get the post showing up for people on this Saturday morning looking for some breakfast or brunch ideas.

In this example, London car wrapper Yiannimize has Hashtagged the make and model of the car in the photo to get it seen by people looking for images of that car (or Mercedes in general). He's also used some more general Instagram tags (#lovecars) and Hashtags used by the wrapping niche (#crazywraps #carwraps #londonwraps), plus his own Hashtag (#yiannimize) to encourage his followers to use that Hashtag in their own posts. The response that his posts get make him one for the Instagram must follow list.

Apps like *Hashtags by PreGram* or *Tags for Likes* will give you a list of popular Hashtags around your subject to get you started. You can use the search feature inside Instagram to find more Hashtags, for example:

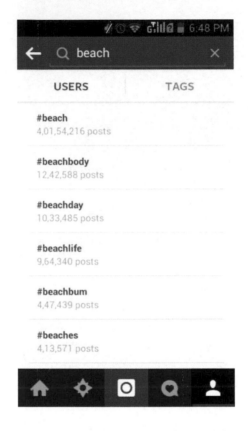

In addition there are lots of generic popular Hashtags that you can use to get more likes. These are so popular that unless your photos are spectacularly dull, you're very likely to pick up at least a few likes from them! Here are the top 20 most popular Instagram Hashtags according to The Huffington Post:

1. #love
2. #instagood
3. #me
4. #tbt
5. #cute
6. #photooftheday
7. #instamood
8. #beautiful
9. #picoftheday
10. #igers
11. #girl
12. #instadaily
13. #iphonesia
14. #follow
15. #tweegram
16. #happy
17. #summer
18. #instagramhub
19. #bestoftheday
20. #iphoneonly

Because Instagram posts are generally ordered by recency, they can suffer the same fate as Tweets and get buried very quickly. This is a particular issue for popular Hashtags, so the most popular will have more specific variations. The tag #chanel has had 2 million posts for example, so if you have some Chanel-inspired earrings for sale, as well as this tag, you might want to add in some more specific ones:

#chanelearrings or #ilovechanel. Keep playing around with different hashtags and search whether they fit with the message you are trying to project. Instagram only allows you to upload 30 hashtags per post, so you have 30 opportunities to pick up some views for each post!

One of the tools that us social media Ninjas love to use alongside Instagram is Iconosquare, a free application that allows you to

- Promote your Instagram accounts across other social networking with feed tabs and photo widgets.
- Manage your community and their comments on a user-friendly platform.
- Analyse your activity through professional statistics.
- Search for users or specific hashtags.
- Launch an Instagram contest in a matter of minutes.

One of the best benefits of Iconosquare is that it allows you to quickly scan your feed. Liking and commenting on your community's videos/pictures is easy because everything is presented on one page for you. Iconosquare also shows your own posts, the likes and/or comments that you've received and more information about your followers. In a sense it's the basic Analytics tool that Instagram itself lacks, and can be a massive time saver.

It's also useful for Hashtag research, making it useful if you have a brand-specific hashtag or if you are running a contest and would like to see the entries. Iconosquare pulls up all the images related to that specific hashtag and organises it all on one page ready for you to like and comment on.

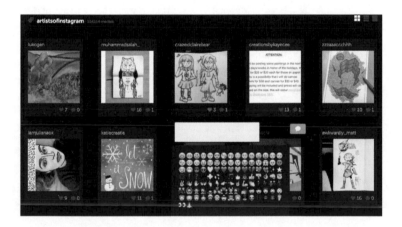

There is also a monthly statistics option that allows you to analyse engagement, content, community and content from the last month.

Re-Posting Content

Whilst Instagram itself doesn't have Repost functionality built in, there are various third party apps that do the job for you and give credit to the original poster. Repost is one of our favourites, and works for photos and videos. Unfortunately the presentation of the photo credit isn't the prettiest, so if you want to repost (and you have the permission of the original poster) the quick and dirty method is to take a screenshot of the post you like on your phone, and crop it to post to your own profile. You can add an @credit in the description to the original poster manually. makes it easy to Repost your favourite photos & videos on Instagram while giving credit to the original Instagrammer.

The slightly less quick and dirty method is to save the original pictures on your computer. Here's how you do it:

- Go to Instagram on your desktop. Right click on the video / picture you want to save.

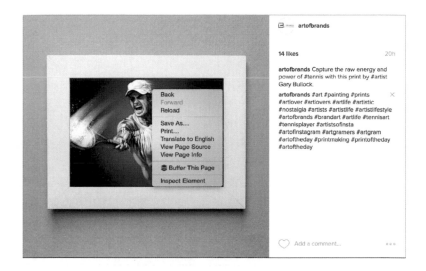

- Click INSPECT ELEMENT
- Look for a link that ends with a .jpg. Click the link (highlighting it) and then copy it. For videos, you should be looking for a link that ends in .mp4. You are specifically looking for an https:// file which has the words src = in front of it.

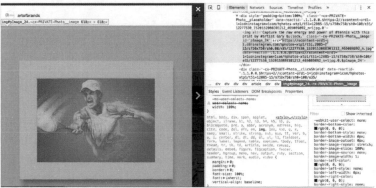

223

- Open a separate window and copy and paste the link in the address bar. The photo or video should appear. Right click and save regularly.

So why would you want to pull videos and photos from other Instagram accounts? Let's go back the example of 'The Ninjas,' an adrenaline-fuelled musical that combines elements of love, loss and digital marketing in a 90-minute emotional rollercoaster. The show runs in four different countries (U.S, Canada, France and England).

The Ninja's social media manager, let's call her Charlotte, is based in their headquarters in Toronto, Ontario and only travels to each of the shows once per year to gather photos and media. Most of the time, media is being sent to her in a very sporadic fashion. There are times when she gets twenty pictures at a time and other days when nothing is being sent to her. Charlotte is incredibly frustrated (can you detect any personal experience here?) and finds herself scrambling to find content to publish every day on Facebook, Twitter and Instagram. But Charlotte notices that the performers from the France and England shows LOVE to post backstage photos and videos of themselves on Instagram while the show-goers in all four countries share hundreds of photos every week. She finds this information by using Iconosquare and typing in the hashtag of the show #TheNinjas, which brings a mixture of videos and photos from performers, backstage crew and show-goers that are spectacular and could be shared on the Ninja's social channels.

So what does Charlotte do?

She sends an email to each of the country's PR coordinators asking them to send an email to all performers and backstage crew about sharing their photos on various social media channels. So instead of waiting for people to send in media, all that a performer needs to do is tag their picture/video with the specific hashtag #TheNinjascrew, which gives Charlotte consent to take and use the photo on the company's main pages (crediting the performer and any other individuals who might appear in the picture). If they forget to add a hashtag, Charlotte simply comments on Instagram photo: "great picture can we use this on our social?" in which the performer answers: "for sure! You can use any of my pictures without any problems." For shower-goers Charlotte does the same thing, asking individuals if she can share the picture on the company's main social media channels. Nine times out ten people agree and Charlotte is now flooded with original and engaging content that costs almost nothing and creates a strong bond between the brand, performers and fans. It's a win-win-win situation!

Instagram Ads

Instagram Ads are managed through Facebook Power Editor, which we covered in the Facebook Ads section of this book. The only difference between posting Facebook Ads and Instagram Ads is the selection of Instagram as the Placement for an Ad Set:

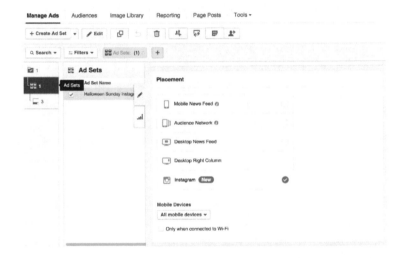

When you post an Instagram ad, you have the option to make the ad appear to be posted by your Instagram page, but only if your Instagram and Facebook accounts are linked:

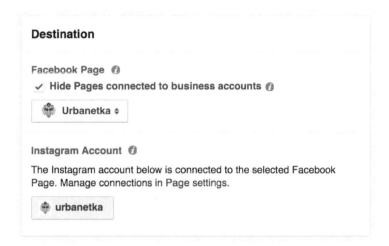

If you don't have an Instagram account or can't link your IG and Facebook Business accounts, you can still run Instagram ads. But without the ads being linked, you won't be able to see any likes or comments generated by the ad run. The downside of this is that you'll often get feedback (good or bad) and questions from Instagrammers on your ads, which you won't be able to respond to.

Aside from using the Instagram Ad platform, you can also advertise through Instagram unofficially. In many markets, professional Instagram marketers maintain popular accounts with the sole purpose of building a large audience to sell advertising to. If they deem your content a good fit for their audience, they'll often sell you exposure in the shape of a featured post.

Buying a featured post on one of these accounts can get you in front of a very large targeted audience, as these profiles can build followings in the hundreds of thousands. The endorsement of such an authority can give you a powerful perception boost, so how do you go about finding suitable opportunities?

Let's use the entrepreneur market as an example. Motivational quotes are a popular type of content on Instagram, and a scan through the most popular posts will regularly show up pictures like this:

It's perfect Instagram fodder for this market: gorgeous aspirational picture paired with a quote. The profile that posted this image is called millionaire_mentor (no prizes for guessing the target audience), who has built

228

a following of over 1.2 *million* followers. This post had 15.3k likes in just one day, so it's safe to say that here we've found a profile with good engagement.

Let's take a look at this profile to see the clues that they might be open to sponsored content:

millionaire_mentor FOLLOWING ▾

Jason Stone · Entrepreneur Lifestyle Publication · Inspiration | Motivation | Success | Resources · MillMentor1@gmail.com · 🐚 30 Successful Business Ideas **bit.ly/FreeBusinessGuide**

191 posts   **1.2m** followers   **389** following

The first clue is that Jason has listed an email address, so is open to contact. The second clue is that there's a download link to a free guide, which is written by an author that doesn't appear to have anything to do with the Instagram account.

The sort of promoted post you might run with millionaire_mentor might look like this:

(Please note that this post is given for illustration only. We don't know whether or not this was a promoted post).

Note that the goal of this post is to boost followers for the @Successtalk profile, and the caption is very much ad copy.

Costs for this type of post vary hugely according to the size of the profiles and the competition in your market, but a ballpark figure for a page with one million followers to run ten posts and leave each one up for an hour (yes, they'll take them down after an hour to prevent their Instagram feed looking too spammy) is $1,000.

Blogging

Your blog will usually be the central focus point for all your social sharing. It's the hub where you'll want to publish your work, and all your social channels feed traffic into it. It's where you publish your ideas, create networking opportunities and boost your website's ranking, all on your own terms.

Yet so few businesses maintain an active blog, typically either treating it as a place to dump SEO content or trying to ignore the fact that their well-intentioned weekly posting schedule got forgotten after three weeks... two years ago.

The hardest part of blogging is starting, and the second hardest part is keeping it going. There always seems to be better things to do, and besides — what could we possibly write about anyway? Who would be interested in what *we* have to say?

These thought seep and put an end to most blogs even before the first key is pressed. I've spoken to countless confident business owners and leaders in their fields who talk about being unable overcome the fear that peers, customers and the wider world will judge their blog. What if the audience doesn't like what they say? What if they make a mistake and look stupid? What if their authority crumbles around them as their blog reveals for the first time that the emperor is, in fact, wearing no clothes? These fears are far from unusual, and almost everyone new to blogging faces them at some point.

The first truth is that any blog is unlikely to get this amount of attention in the early days. Unless you are already extremely high profile, your blog is unlikely to make a significant dent in the universe for the first 5 posts, so you have a bit of time to find your feet. The second truth is that these worries are exactly the same worries that everyone else shares. Almost everyone who decided to build their own profile faced the same worries when they started. The difference between the winner and the loser is deciding to go for it anyway, whilst competitors remain paralysed by the fear of their blog becoming fantastically popular.

So let's assume that you'll put any fears aside, accept that your blog will never be perfect and that you'll continue to improve and develop your own style as you go. The pressure is now off, let's get started.

Getting Started with Blogging

Your business blog will form the foundation of your social media presence, so it's important to have a plan before you set off.

Step 1 - Choose the focus of your blog:

And no, "writing about our company" is not a suitable focus! Exactly *who* are you writing for, and what do they need? How can you move them closer to their goals whilst positioning your business as the solution to their problems, and dropping in mentions of your products or services in a natural way?

One of our clients sells cruises and they run a fantastic blog, written by their staff, talking about all of the destinations, ports, ships and cruise companies that their cruises feature. This is genuinely useful to cruise shoppers, because these staff are all cruise experts. An honest opinion from someone who has been on dozens of cruises holds some weight.

Another client runs a holiday lettings business. Their blog talks about the region, things to do, holiday packages, and anything that holidaymakers would need to know about a trip to the area.

If you're unsure what your audience likes to read about, check out the sort of articles that run in the magazines and blogs they read. Look at the sort of content they share and Retweet, and in particular anything that gets an emotional response (either positive or negative).

Your staff might be expert in topics that your audience would love to read up on, but you have no idea about. Remember that you don't have to write this blog alone, and giving team members a platform to share the expertise they've built up can be good for both you and them.

Step 2 - Pick a platform:

If you already have a website with a built-in blog (for example Wordpress), then the decision about which platform to use is easy. Having a built-in blog is usually preferable because it makes navigation between your blog and website straightforward, and means that the look and feel remains consistent throughout.

If your website *doesn't* and *can't* have a blog built in, you'll need to choose a separate blogging platform. For ease of use sake, we tend to recommend Wordpress. The range of plugins (to add functionality), the simplicity of creating and editing posts, and the SEO friendliness make it the logical choice in the vast majority of cases.

Wordpress blogs come in two flavours: hosted and self-hosted. *Self-hosted* blogs live on your own hosting, whereas *hosted* blogs live on Wordpress servers. You have more control over a self-hosted Wordpress blog - including over things like the domain name, layout, and use of plugins for additional functionality - so this is usually the most appropriate option. The downside is that setting up a self-hosted Wordpress blog takes longer and requires more technical ability than setting up a hosted one, and you'll be responsible for the ongoing maintenance. Self-hosted Wordpress is a free download from www.wordpress.org.

Hosted blogs on the other hand (www.wordpress.com, Tumblr or Google's Blogger, for example) are much simpler to set up and even someone with no prior experience can be happily blogging away in a matter of minutes. The downside is that you sacrifice many of the customisation features of a self-hosted blog in return for the convenience. Even if you pay to upgrade your hosted blog, you'll still not have the level of control that a free self-hosted blog gives you.

There are plenty of free instructions to take you through the process of setting up a Wordpress blog on your own hosting, and if you get stuck your hosting provider will be able to provide support. Of course, we're happy to help where we can too, so feel free to drop an email to support@exposureninja.com if you get stuck.

Step 3 - Branding your blog:

It's important that your blog and your website share the same branding to give a feeling of coherence. Most blog platforms will give you space to put a logo and choose the colours used, at the least. Any customisation beyond that is down to the particular platform and theme that you're using.

Remember that perception is 90% of the game in social media, and it's important that your blog looks the part if you want to build credibility. Having a professional designer create the graphics and layout for your blog can be a wise investment if it saves you hours battling the settings yourself, only to get it looking 5/10. Just as with your main website, you've got to be really honest with yourself about whether your blog looks professional enough. You need to appear world class, so your website and blog should look world class.

Step 4 - Planning your content:

We looked at audience profiling earlier in this book, and clearly this is the first step for any targeted marketing effort, including blogging. The topics you cover in your blog need to be the topics that your audience really cares about. When we're working with a client new to blogging, we'll ask them to list out common questions or misunderstandings that their audience has about the product, service or need. Each of these questions can be the basis of at least one blog post.

Each question becomes a blog post title. The blog posts themselves are just the most perfect answers to each question that you can write. Do this ten times, and you should already have the most useful blog in your market.

Blogs often use categories to sort their content, and you can map these categories out to help you think of more blog post topics. A personal trainer might use *fat loss*, *building muscle, workout tips, supplements, diet, health* and *sleep* as their main categories, because they know that these are the broad topics their audience is interested in. Now when they're stuck for blog content to write, they can just look through their list of categories and think up the questions their audience might have around each topic. This category approach removes the scary 'blank page syndrome' and gives you a starting point from which to build. At the time of writing this chapter, my personal trainer (Dan Smith from M10 Fitness) is currently struggling to think up blog topics. Let's continue the example above to see if we can help him out. We'll just start with the sleep category, and see if we can list some of the most common questions people might have about sleep (you can use Google to help find common questions too):

1. How much sleep do I need?
2. How long before bed should I eat?
3. How long before bed should I work out?
4. What should my sleep routine look like?
5. Do you have any tips for more restful sleep?
6. Are there supplements that are good for sleep?
7. What time should I wake up?
8. Is it OK to lie in or does that mess up my body clock?
9. How can I stop myself from waking up in the night?
10. My fitbit tells me that my sleep is not restful - what's up?
11. Why do I snore?
12. What sort of mattress should I have?
13. What sort of pillow should I have?

… And so on. So right there are thirteen blog post topics from just *one* of the seven categories we identified. Assuming we can find twenty common questions about each category, we have ourselves a hundred and forty blog posts in the pipeline. You'd better start writing Dan!

Remember too that you don't have to create all the content on your blog yourself. If someone in your team has more time and they know what they're talking about, outsourcing the writing to them can free you up.

Maybe you've already tried blogging before and, for whatever reason, the momentum just stopped? It's a common problem and the solution is to create a content schedule. Whether you want to blog daily, weekly or monthly, committing yourself to a particular date and time in the diary where you'll sit down and come up with a new blog post - even planning what you'll be writing in that session beforehand to give your subconscious some time to collect ideas - can be the key to keeping your energy up and your blog alive. If it gets left until you have some spare time, it won't get done. It needs to be on the priority list.

Using visual content

Using pictures, videos, gifs and Tweets in your blog posts makes them much more interesting, boosts time on page (how long people spend reading the blog), and increases your social shares. Posts with pictures get more space and better visibility on Facebook, so make sure each post's featured image in particular is eye catching. The featured image is usually the one that Facebook will show when someone shares your blog post, so it's effectively a picture headline for the content.

In general it's best to avoid stock photos that are *clearly* stock photos. Instead opt for higher quality stock images (such as those from dollarphotoclub or deathtothestockphoto), or original images. The pictures you use throughout your blog posts should be consistent and appropriate to your business: a local plumber will find that iPhone pictures of recent plumbing jobs give him or her a lot more credibility amongst their audience than corporate stock photos, whereas a large multinational training company would be expected to use professionally taken *original* photos.

If you're struggling to identify the sort of pictures that will most suit your blog posts, think about what your solution represents to your customers. Peace of mind, saving time, happy relationships, physical health and financial success are all 'towards' motivators that can be easily represented by images. Or perhaps your customers have a significant source of 'away from' motivation such as legal issues, physical or mental pain, financial trouble, unhappiness or rejection. What sort of images would illustrate these for your audience?

Blogging SEO

Aside from giving us the opportunity to drive qualified social media traffic to your site, blogging also brings with it the opportunity to boost your website's ranking on Google and other search engines. We take an in-depth look at SEO in our #1 best selling SEO title: How To Get To The Top Of Google, but for now let's look at how you can use Ninja SEO principles to increase the ranking of your blog.

Keywords

Keywords are the words and phrases your audience uses to search for your product, service or benefit. For example, a women's shoe shop might sell a range of sandals for weddings. After talking to their customers and doing some research online, the owner identifies that "white wedding sandals" is one of the phrases her audience uses. It matches with their most popular shoes in this category so the decision is made to target the phrase "white wedding sandals" by writing a blog post called "The Perfect White Wedding Sandals". This post could talk about recent trends in wedding footwear, the particular white wedding sandals on sale, and important considerations when choosing a pair. The words "white", "wedding" and "sandals", the phrase "white wedding sandals" and related phrases such as "white wedding shoes" would appear throughout the blog post giving Google and the other search engines a really clear idea that this post is about white wedding sandals, and significantly increase the blog's visibility for this phrase on Google.

By spending the time to understand the sort of keywords your audience uses, you can construct blog posts targeting these phrases, giving you more chance of showing up for them on Google. Here are some more tips on getting the most out of keywords:

- **Specific is good:** By focusing on a narrowly targeted set of keywords ("White wedding sandals" rather than the more generic and competitive "wedding shoes"), you make it more likely that your posts will rank highly in search engines. Consider also the *commercial intent* of these keywords: people searching for "white wedding sandals" are likely to be more ready to buy than those searching for "wedding shoes", who are probably still in the research phase because they haven't yet identified the type of shoes they're looking for.
- **Use your keywords in the post title:** Titles have a huge importance in SEO, so including your keywords in your title (and towards the start of the title, if possible) will help boost your ranking, as well as show your audience clearly what your post is about.
- **Use the right keyword density in the blog post:** Thanks to the rise of semantic search, the days of needing to *stuff* your blog post full of keywords are over. Of course you'll still want to make sure your keywords are used

throughout, but be natural with your language, and make sure to include variations and related phrases too because this gives Google a broader understand of what your post is about. As for length, aim to make your blog posts at least 300 words, but don't be afraid to go much longer - as long as the content justifies it.

- **Use internal links:** Whenever a blog post is shared on social media, the chances are that people will be landing on your website from that post. If they land on that blog post page, how do you plan to turn them into a customer, or get them to stay and take a look around your site? We have one client who, despite being a very smart marketer, hadn't thought this through. We noticed that his website's blog posts had a very high bounce rate - in other words people were coming in from social media and then leaving. He was getting plenty of visitors because he chose great blog post topics and the quality of his posts was high. But these visitors just weren't spending any time on the rest of the site. After running some tests we established that because there was no call to action and no internal links in the posts, visitors were reading them, getting what they needed, and heading straight back to Facebook. To counteract this, we put links to other pages on his site (called internal links) throughout the blog posts. When the blog mentioned a service that the company

243

offered, we put a link to that service. This got people clicking around the site and discovering how the business could help them. It reduced his bounce rate and increased traffic to the other pages. Any time you mention one of your products or services in a blog post, include a link to the relevant page so that readers can get more information about it.

- **Use image alt tags:** Image alt tags are used to tell search engines and accessibility software what a picture is about. It's SEO best practice to optimise your image alt tags by writing descriptions of what is shown in each image, using your keywords where possible. How you add your tags will depend on your blog set up. In Wordpress you will see a title and description setting each time you add a picture to your blog post.

Metadata

Most blog platforms allow you to add a meta description to your posts. This meta description is often shown on Google and social media as the description of the post. If you think about it, this makes it the second most important piece of text on your page, other than the title, because it's essentially an advert to get people onto your site in the first place.

A good Meta description contains up to 160 characters and arouses curiosity to make people click. Unlike the Page Title, Google doesn't use the keywords used in the Meta description as a ranking indicator, but it's still a good idea to include them because those are the words your audience is tuned to look out for, having just searched for them.

In the screenshot below you'll see the SEO settings screen of the Wordpress SEO by Yoast plugin. This screen shows the general Title and Meta description, which are the ones used by Google.

You'll notice that there is a tab marked 'Social' along the top. This allows you to set separate titles, descriptions and images to show up when the article is shared on Facebook and Twitter. The description you use for Facebook can be slightly longer (we recommend 200 characters, although Facebook will

245

show up to 300). Twitter's description is limited to 200 characters.

When choosing a photo to show with your blog posts on Facebook or Twitter, use a 1024 x 512 image, which is a good ratio for both networks. Keep in mind that any text used in the image needs to be in the centre, because Facebook will likely crop off the top and bottom, like this:

If you need a tool to quickly generate amazing looking pictures for social media, check out Canva in our Tools section later on.

The Power of a Good Blog Post Headline

We've covered headlines elsewhere in this book, and the basic principles of writing a good one apply whether we're talking about a blog post headline, Tweet, Facebook post or Instagram bio. Your audience will usually decide whether or not to click on your blog posts based on the headline alone. If you want your blog posts to attract viral spread, the headlines you use are absolutely crucial because they determine how many people click on the article, which determines how visible it is, which determines how often it is shared. Good headlines get you on the way to viral spread. Bad headlines, no matter how good the post, will never get you the visibility you need.

Some examples of good headlines that use a mixture of curiosity and, yes, a little sensationalism to brighten up some potentially boring subjects:

- 6 Unbelievable Personal Injury Claims
- At First, I Felt Sorry For The People Who Live In This Tiny House. Then I Looked Closer...Now I'm Jealous.
- Britain: Bankrupt by 2017?

- He's Trying To Make Buses Sexy, And It's Working
- Canada's Response To Russia's Anti-LGBT Propaganda Law Is Totally Awesome
- College degrees with the highest starting salaries
- Eight surprising ways to increase productivity in the workplace
- Empty Pigs: Why banks have given up on savers
- Starbucks asks customers to leave their guns at home

Most of these are taken from viral sites like Buzzfeed, who have grown their entire business on tapping into viral spread due largely to the quality of their headlines.

So what's the secret to writing a good headline? The most viral worthy headlines (and all of the above) use a 'curiosity gap'. They leave the reader with an open loop in their head that they just *have* to close: "tiny house? I wonder what it looks like and why people are jealous of it?" The point of the headline is to sell the *click*. Once the visitor is on the page, the images and content have to keep them there.

Many of them also skillfully use emotion, whether it's fear ("Britain: Bankrupt by 2017?") or anger ("Empty Pigs: why banks have given up on savers").

Headline writing is part art, part science and part relentless determination. You're unlikely to smash it out of the park in your first attempt, and in fact if it takes you twenty attempts to get one you like, you're doing better than some of the world's best writers; Upworthy requires its writers to 'crap out' 25 headlines for every good one they write.

Growing Your Blog Audience

Your blog's goal is to attract new readers, build familiarity with them and turn some into customers. So let's take a look at some ways to promote your blog to get it a bigger audience.

Encourage Social Media Sharing: Any time that your success is dependent on your audience taking initiative or going out of their way to help, you are doomed to failure. So make it *brain dead* easy for your readers to share your blog posts on social media with one click, by putting social sharing buttons right alongside the blog posts themselves. Use www.clicktoTweet.com to make it easy to share your most Tweetable content too — the more barriers you can remove, the more shares you'll attract.

To collect the email addresses of your readers, consider offering an email subscription option that allows people to automatically receive your new blog posts. Then make the email subscription even more appealing by offering an additional incentive to get the signup, such as a free email course, exclusive video or something else that costs you little to deliver but has high perceived value. And of course, make it as simple as possible to sign up: the more you force people to work for the subscription, the fewer will bother.

Popups such as those from Popup Domination annoy visitors but they *do* convert well, so if your business relies on building a large email list it's worth considering this sort of conversion device.

Market Your Blog Posts on Your Own Social Channels: Once you've created your keyword-optimised blog post with pictures, a great headline and share buttons, it's time to get promoting it on your own channels. Linking to your post from your company Facebook, Twitter, Google+ and Linkedin accounts can all bring you valuable traffic. If your content is very visual, posting pictures from your blog post on Pinterest can be another great source of visitors, as the pictures will automatically link back to your blog.

Don't be afraid to outreach to industry figures, customers and peers asking for feedback on your post as well. If they like what they read and decide to share it, this can generate valuable referral traffic, which you can then convert to regular visitors.

In addition to your own profiles on other social networks, there are some other neat strategies for promoting your content:

1. **Publish your blog on Kindle and get paid!** Head to https://kindlepublishing.amazon.com and sign up to publish your blog on Amazon's Kindle platform. While this won't be a huge source of revenue for anyone but the most high profile bloggers, it *can* be a good way to find new readers.

2. **Paid Content Syndication:** Outbrain.com, DemandStudios.com and other content syndication platforms allow you to pay to promote your blog posts on well-known sites. Paid advertising can be a fast way to attract new blog readers, but before putting too much cash into advertising we recommend building up a following organically in order to prove that your posts are share-worthy, interesting and relevant enough to your audience that they will subscribe. Trying to paper over cracks with high advertising spend can be a costly route to failure so it's best to make sure your blog is working well for you with your existing channels first.

3. **Guest Posting:** Guest posting involves writing blog posts for other sites in order to get in front of their audience. We regularly secure guest

posting opportunities for our clients as it's a great way to piggyback authority sites with established audiences. Each post should be unique and targeted at the blog's native audience and reflect the sort of interests they have. If in doubt, ask the blog owner to suggest a topic that they think their audience would be interested in reading about. Good guests posts aren't overly pitchy or promotional, but you'll want to include a link back to your blog in the article body as well as the bio/signature area. We look at guest posting outreach in more detail in How To Get To The Top Of Google.

4. **Advertising on Social Media:** If your blog posts are really high value, running some paid ads to drive traffic to them can give you feedback on how likely readers are to signup for your service or join your email list. If you've got a Facebook pixel installed on your site, you can run retargeting ads to these visitors to bring them back for more blog posts or some lead generation bait.

How often should you blog?

It's one of the most common questions and the answer is simple: as often as your schedule allows. As a minimum, any business that wants to generate a significant social audience for their posts should be blogging at least once per week, but 2-3 times per week is better, and every day is best if you have the capacity.

If you're a larger company with staff, there is no reason not to up the frequency even further. One of our clients, having seen the effect their blog had on their traffic, decided to get their team involved and now posts multiple times per day. Their competitors can't match the frequency or quality of the posts, so on social media the difference between the buzzing, popular and productive business and their sluggish and silent competitors is striking. By writing blogs targeting every imaginable question and topic their audience could think of, they've cast a very wide net and this has significantly boosted their SEO visibility too.

Types of Blog Post

As well as the standard question/answer blog post structure, there are other formats that your blogs can take:

Instructional

Is there something technical that you can provide a walkthrough guide for? Can you show your visitors how to do something that they might otherwise struggle with? If you decide to video your walkthrough, it's a good idea to write the instructions out too (with screenshots if it's online) so that people (and Google!)

who want to follow the text can understand what's going on as well.

Reviews

If you're an e-commerce business and the products you sell don't already have reviews, consider writing your own in-depth reviews and posting these on your blog. Video reviews are a fantastic asset for any e-commerce site, and as well as writing up blog posts from the videos you can include them directly on your product pages.

If your business offers an alternative to an established competitor, you can write a post about the differences between your offerings. Targeting a phrase like "<Competitor> alternative" can get you visibility on Google in front of people who need something similar but are looking for someone else cheaper, better or with slightly different functionality.

Research & studies

If you conduct research or carry out studies, this sort of original material makes perfect blog posts and is ideal fodder for social sharing. If you don't yet conduct studies, what sort of insights might your audience would be interested in learning about? A study doesn't have to be expensive or painful to conduct: a Google form and respondents sourced from Amazon Mechanical Turk is the quickest way to get up and running and can generate you some insights within a couple of days.

Infographics

An infographic is a visual way to present statistics, instructions or any other information that can be presented in a visual way. Infographics exploded in popularity because they make perfect social sharing material, and they're fairly simple to build. Piktochart and Canva both offer Infographic design software, or you can find a designer that specialises in Infographics to get something a bit more tailored.

Some quick tips to help you make your Infographics as effective as possible:
- Keep your Infographic simple: if in doubt, leave it out. You want people to feel drawn in by the promise of quick, attractive information. If your infographic is very long and contains lots of small point text, you'll have a tough time encouraging readers to invest the time even to start reading it.
- Give it a killer title. Just like any content online, the title is the advert for the Infographic. Use something snappy and make it appeal to your target audience, then stick the title nice and large at the top.
- Make the colours bold, bright and attractive, and make sure that all text is easy to read. Use

high contrast colour combinations for text to make your Infographic readable for those on lower-quality screens.

- Plan your visitor's 'flow' through the Infographic. You can use a graphical 'path' or a line that leads readers from one section to the next, without them wandering off-piste and getting lost.

Blogging Summary

There is no question that every business that wants to boost their social visibility needs to run an active blog. It gives you a hub to promote your content from, draws people to your website, boosts your ranking and increases your perceived authority. Yes, it takes some work to write the posts but it doesn't have to be you that does this work! Passionate staff, or a company like Exposure Ninja experienced in running blogs can handle the legwork, leaving you to get on with running the business.

Create a content schedule, write some post titles, diarise them, and stick to these appointments if you want to get your blog off to a great start. And if you really can't face it, contact us and we can handle it all for you.

LinkedIn

LinkedIn is the business-oriented social network of choice for most professionals. There are now over 400 million active users, with two new users signing up every second. Long used by recruiters and headhunters, recent research has shown that some employers look at LinkedIn profiles *before* reading resumes, indicating just how deeply it has penetrated the world of business. With 2.6 million companies already having their own LinkedIn page, it all presents a pretty compelling argument for getting involved, although we've certainly found it to be more productive in some markets than others.

What sort of opportunities are available to small and medium-sized businesses on the network, and what sort of companies stand to benefit the most?

On the whole, most of the businesses that use LinkedIn for marketing tend to be B2B, because that's the frame of mind LinkedIn users have whilst they're using the site. That doesn't mean that it *can't* be profitable for B2C companies, but work-related products and services do tend to find greater success.

Similarly to Facebook, LinkedIn marketing for businesses is done via a business profile page. Through this page you can post status updates, link to content (both on LinkedIn and elsewhere on the web), and share your job openings. It's safe to say that the company profile has taken some cues from Facebook business pages, and the same interaction options (like, share & comment) are available to your audience. If you're new to LinkedIn marketing but have experience with Facebook, it will all feel very familiar.

Your Company's Voice

Because people tend to be in a business frame of mind when using LinkedIn, the tone of business posts tends to be more professional, conservative and, well, business-like. Engagement levels also tend to be (on the whole) lower, so don't judge your page a failure if you don't get the sort of sharing, liking and commenting activity that you're used to receiving on Facebook.

This doesn't mean that your audience won't respond to the same psychological triggers that they'll respond to on any of the other networks though. Catchy post headlines, compelling pictures and concise descriptions will do well no matter the audience or the channel. Your business personality still needs to come across in everything you write, and you can never afford be boring.

LinkedIn Pulse

Think of Pulse as a blog you can contribute to, hosted on LinkedIn. Because LinkedIn wants to be a place that influencers demonstrate their influence, it's important that the network gives influential users a soapbox to stand on. So whilst Facebook has posts, Twitter has Tweets and Instagram has pictures, LinkedIn wants to get its members posting on Pulse.

The good news is that if your audience is B2B, the chances are that there is a proportion of your market that spends a good amount of time on LinkedIn interacting with content that they find.

What sort of content do users of LinkedIn respond best to? According to LinkedIn's own study, six out of ten LinkedIn users are interested in industry insights, with 53% interested in company news. Can you scratch this itch? What sort of insights do you have in your arsenal, and how could you present them so that the post is most likely to get clicks? If you have company news, make sure that it's genuinely interesting to your audience: a new product is never as exciting to your audience as it is to your team, so how can you tie the topic into something with broader appeal that'll be more likely to get you shares and exposure?

Post frequency is an important visibility factor. LinkedIn's own 'Sophisticated Marketer's guide to

LinkedIn' found that twenty posts per month is optimum for high visibility (reaching on average 60% of your audience), with some marketers posting as many as 3-4 posts per day.

Unless you've found LinkedIn to be a primary source of new business, this level of activity is usually not practical for most SMEs, and the pressure to post *more* stuff should never get in the way of posting *great* stuff.

Formatting Your Post

When it comes to posting content on LinkedIn, best practice guidelines closely mirror blogging best practice. We'll look in more detail at blogging later on, but for now here are some quick tips:

- A good LinkedIn post starts with a good title. Make it short but descriptive, and leave out enough to intrigue your readers to click on the post to find out more.
- You'll want to use a good header image as this functions like a Facebook cover photo for your post, but remember that you can also embed images *throughout* the article to break up the text and keep your audience interested.
- If you can embed rich media (videos, Slideshare presentations etc.) in a natural way, this is also a good idea. Opera Mediaworks reports that videos attract as much as four times the engagement of static images.

- Keep your post length to between 500-100 words. According to a study by Brian Lang (http://www.smallbusinessideasblog.com/linkedin-publishing), posts of this length are the most likely to be featured on Pulse.

Promoting Your Post

LinkedIn's visibility algorithm takes into consideration not *how many views* your post has had, but how often they are liked and shared, *relative* to the number of views. In other words the virality of your post defines how much visibility it gets. There are a lot of positive feedback loops on social media, and this is one of them!

To get your post off to a good start, first make sure that you're posting it at an optimal time. Generally avoid weekends and late afternoons, as LinkedIn's audience is thinking about other things during this time. Once you've posted your piece, share it through your other social channels and, if you've got an email list, consider sending out a link. Remember that although you usually want to post original content to your own blog rather than driving traffic to somebody else's site (in this case LinkedIn), we're doing this specifically to get some visibility across the LinkedIn network. Good early interaction with your article — driven by existing contacts — can launch you to wider exposure, so occasionally giving your best work to another platform other than your own website is sometimes worth the tradeoff.

Using LinkedIn Discussion Groups

LinkedIn Discussion Groups can be a fantastic way of collecting leads, peers, customers or just about anyone else. Similar in principle to Google+ Communities covered elsewhere in this book, LinkedIn groups warrant some serious study for businesses that have a significant potential business audience.

There are already thousands of specialist groups for every industry, sector or problem imaginable (and plenty that are unimaginable), but starting your own group can give you perceived authority and clout, which you can use to your advantage later on.

One of our clients (a recruitment training business) wanted to promote a webinar we were running together. We sent the boss over to LinkedIn and told him to start making a name for himself in discussion groups, in order to build an audience. From calling out established industry figures to predicting future trends and generally stirring up controversy, he made as much noise as he possibly could in as many relevant groups as he could find. Once the group members were familiar with him and he'd been active in some of the hottest conversations, he set up his own group and began to invite members over. The response was great and owning the group boosted his credibility further with this audience. The experience he gained from studying the previous groups meant he was able to identify a new angle for his own group, which he built up and began using to promote the online events, as well as his books and courses.

Many groups on LinkedIn are set to Private, with new members requiring approval from the group manager. Generally these groups tend to be higher quality because irrelevant members are filtered out and the group retains a high level of integrity.

To begin boosting your visibility in LinkedIn discussion groups, join any that you can find in your market and jump in with both feet, adding to the discussions, asking questions and offering your opinion when relevant. Spend some time observing which groups are the most active, why, and notice the types of post that tend to drive high interaction. All of this is useful research for your own group and will help you hit the ground running. It also gives you a chance to build relationships with some of the most prominent figures in the LinkedIn groups, whose authority you can then piggyback.

If you're relatively new to LinkedIn and would like to find some suitable groups to join, you can start by typing keywords into the search bar and choosing Groups from the menu. The search results will show you the largest and most active groups that those in your network are a part of, and you can follow this paper trail to find groups with a suitable level of activity in topics relevant to you.

Starting Your Own LinkedIn Group

When the time comes for you to start your own group, choose Groups from the Interests menu at the top of the page, and click the button to Create a new group. On the set up page you'll see options for naming your group, writing the description and giving a URL as well as setting the picture and choosing whether the group is closed (new members require approval and discussions aren't publicly visible) or open (new members can join instantly and all discussions are public).

If your main goal is to raise visibility, then creating an open group is usually the best option because people won't need to wait for your approval to jump in.

When deciding the focus of your group, you'll need to balance having a wide net to attract enough members with focusing the group enough that it has value for the members and the discussions don't become too off-topic. The group name and logo will be the most visible components across LinkedIn, so people should be able to understand immediately what the group is about from just the title alone. Avoid use of your company name unless it is a genuine attraction to potential customers, as this gives the game away without much of a fight!

Just as with the other social media marketing strategies in this book, seek to add value to the group/market/audience *first*. Once people are familiar with you, they'll be far more responsive to any marketing messages you push out. If you're the group facilitator, there's a perceived authority that is very powerful and gives you a high level of credibility, but that authority must be used wisely and sparingly. Pitching your group members before you have the credibility to do so in a compelling way is such bad form. You've likely been to network events and met the person carrying round a handful of their own business cards ready to thrust into the hand of anyone that inadvertently catches their eye. These people take more than they give, and our social awareness means we see through it immediately.

LinkedIn Advertising

LinkedIn's advertising platform, like its profiles, is quite similar to Facebook. The data it has on its users is more work-oriented so the employment targeting options available are much richer. A lot of the advertising done on LinkedIn is recruitment, but that doesn't stop other businesses from targeting the

LinkedIn audience whether selling consultancy, events, marketing help or even franchises.

It's not just businesses that are already successful with LinkedIn who are able to attract leads and customers from the ad platform either. Experimentation and testing is the only reliable way to find out if, and how well, LinkedIn ads can work for your business.

Let's go through the process of setting up a LinkedIn advertising campaign for the first time:

- To sign up for advertising, go to linkedin.com/ads and click on the 'Start Now' button. You'll see the option to create an ad or promote an update. For this example we'll be creating an ad.
- Before setting up your campaign, decide whether you're advertising a business or yourself. If you're advertising on behalf of your business, you'll want to set up a Business Advertising account by clicking the drop down menu in the top right hand corner. If your company is already on LinkedIn, you can link it at this stage as well as choose your currency.
- You'll need to choose a name for your ad campaign, select the destination (whether you're sending the audience to your website or a page on LinkedIn), then it's time to create your ad

- The rules here are exactly the same as for Facebook: the picture matters, as it's the element that will draw the visitor's eye. Then they'll scan the headline for a perceived benefit. Remember to be clear about benefits and what will happen when they click on the ad.
- Image size is 50x50px and it's important to add a picture, as ads with an image are 20% more likely to be clicked on.
- The ad headline length is a maximum of 25 characters with the ad body allowing 75 characters.
- Once you've written your ad, you can click Duplicate to create a duplicate version, allowing you to test a different image and/or copy. If you're undecided between two pictures, for example, you can test the click through rates using each, thus allowing your audience to choose.

Once you're done setting up your ad, click Next to move to the targeting options....

Targeting Your Audience

The targeting options available include:

- Geography: From targeting continents to specific cities, the geo targeting allows physical shops and businesses serving a specific location to keep their advertising costs economical.

- Company: You can target specific companies by name (useful for laser targeting high value potential clients) or companies by category (size or industry). If you know your audience really well, now you can target them precisely.
- Job Titles: Again, if you know who in your target organisations is responsible for the buying decision, you can narrow your ad focus onto them using the job title targeting. There's no need to waste money advertising to lower level workers if it's upper level management who will be making a decision!
- Groups: you can choose which groups on LinkedIn you'd like to target. There are tens of thousands of groups on LinkedIn ranging from groups regarding a product development inside a company to a company's official group to post job openings etc. You might want to do some research on the groups you'd like to target before adding them. It is a time consuming task but it narrows down your target audience effectively.
- Skills: For LinkedIn advertising, targeting by skills is almost the equivalent of targeting Facebook ads by interest. If your audience is primarily accountants, you can choose 'accountants' in the skills section to narrow your ad visibility to target only those who match your ideal customer.

- Gender and age targeting hopefully need little explanation!
- The last option 'also reach LinkedIn members on other websites through LinkedIn Audience Network' gives your ads legs outside the LinkedIn site. This checkbox gives permission for your ads to be shown on websites that are connected to LinkedIn or show LinkedIn content. If a user is signed up in their LinkedIn account while visiting one of those sites, they can see a personalised ad if they fall into your targeted audience criteria you just set.

So your ad and variations are set, your audience is targeted and it's time to get down to the money...

Budget and Billing

Ads on LinkedIn can get expensive quite quickly. Generally the Cost Per Click (CPC) is a multiple of what Facebook charges, probably due to the quality of the audience. But this means that keeping a close eye on budget is advisable, particularly with new and untested campaigns.

There are two payment options in LinkedIn:
- Pay-per-click (CPC): with this option, you specify the maximum amount of money you're willing to pay each time someone clicks on the ad. This option is a good bet if you're not sure how many people will click on the ad or what

your conversion rate is, because you only pay for real ad clicks.

- Pay-per-1000 impressions (CPM): There are two scenarios when CPM is a good choice:
    a. When you want to 'spread awareness' and don't care too much about how many people click on the ad. This is similar to display advertising where you're paying for the visibility rather than the clicks themselves
    b. If you have a well-performing ad campaign and are generating a lot of clicks, it can sometimes work out cheaper to choose a CPM payment model if you can get more clicks per 1,000 impressions than the industry average.
- You'll then get to set your daily budget, stopping you from being *too* liable should you forget to turn off the ads.
- Minimum costs (in US Dollars. For local currency a rough conversion is done by LinkedIn):
    a. Minimum daily budget is $10/day.
    b. Minimum CPC bid is $2/click.
    c. Minimum CPM bid is $2/1000 impressions.
- If your ad campaign is seeking to generate high quality leads that you can follow up with by email, the Lead Collection option is a neat trick.

This allows your audience to click on the ad to agree to share their contact details with you. You're then notified by email that they've shared their details with you and you can contact them by email or through LinkedIn to tell them more about your business or service.

- There's a starting fee associated with launching a LinkedIn ad campaign of $5 (again, roughly converted to local currency) that becomes ad credit once the campaign is live.

LinkedIn Summary

Generally, we find that the businesses who will do the best already *know* that they'll do well - either their competitors are extremely active, or their industry is well known for spending a lot of time on LinkedIn (for example recruitment). If we could only take three social networks to our social media-marketing island, LinkedIn wouldn't make the cut thanks to its expensive ads and generally lower-than average engagement levels, but that doesn't mean that you shouldn't be testing it. Usually you'll find your competitors aren't, so if you can generate customers at a reasonable cost you'll have a profitable channel that they won't be watching as closely as Facebook, Twitter or Instagram.

New Kids on the Block: Snapchat, Periscope and Beyond…

In the last couple of years two things have been happening: firstly, video has become vastly more popular, not least because faster data connections have meant that slow loading videos are now (mostly) a thing of the past. Secondly, people are becoming overwhelmed with meticulously created content, and the popularity of "real-time" experiences has increased.

We have seen a strong push for video on all channels. Videos that are uploaded directly to Facebook, for example, are more likely to receive organic views than if you post a link to a Youtube video because Facebook wants to own that video content. In 2015, Twitter introduced video, allowing people to shoot, edit and upload video straight from their mobile and in the second half of 2015, Facebook pushed boundaries again with video by allowing brands to post 360° videos for an immersive viewing experience.

But we've also seen a new breed of video-based social networks explode in popularity, such as Meerkat, Periscope and Snapchat.

Live Streaming Apps

Meerkat & Periscope allow you to live stream what is going on around you at any given moment. In simpler terms if Twitter gave people a megaphone, these apps give you a camera crew. Meerkat was released in April 2015, and one month later Twitter introduced Periscope, after announcing that it had bought the company in January 2015. When Periscope launched, Twitter removed its support for Meerkat meaning cutting off some of the features that were previously available to Meerkat users, like creating a map of friends right away and receiving Twitter push notifications when friends begin broadcasting. As a result, many deciding between the two platforms choose Periscope primarily due to the fact that Twitter supports it.

For this chapter we've decided to focus solely on Periscope as statistics show that it's more popular, and we feel it's more likely to succeed long-term.

What Sort Of Content Works Best On Live Streaming Apps?

Live-streaming is fantastic for exclusive and backstage content for your fans and customers; content like photo shoots, ambassador interviews, conferences/panel discussions, product demonstrations/reviews, shop and retail tours, press day access and of course behind the scenes action. Currently most popular for personal brands, or business figures that rely on their personal popularity, let's look at commonalities and lessons from those that are succeeding early on:

1. **Be real and wing it.** The whole point of live streaming (and the key USP of an app like Periscope) is that the content is unscripted and raw that shows something 'real'. It's important to embrace that aspect and avoid pre-scripted and fake live streams. If people wanted scripted, they'd go to YouTube.
2. **Pick the right title.** Your followers see the title of your stream before they decide whether or not to watch. Your title can be either straight forward ("Walking Around in the CN Tower), Exclusive ("Backstage Peak of London Fashion Week) and/or Unique/Weird ("100 viewers and I'll eat a bug"). Even if you don't have a plan for what you'll be streaming, it helps to have some sort of connecting theme so that your audience can see a benefit to tuning in.
3. **Make your broadcast easy to find.** Periscope gives you the option to turn on Twitter sharing, so that when you begin your broadcast it will be shared with your Twitter followers. Also turn on Location Tagging so that people can find you if they are browsing through the "global" function on their Periscope app.
4. **Say hi!** As people start joining your conversation, you'll see notifications in your stream. Make sure to acknowledge them by their Twitter handle.

5. **Ask questions.** Twitter is all about sparking conversations and Periscope is no different. Ask your viewers questions like "what would you guys like to see next?" or something as simple as "does anyone want to ask me anything?" Viewers will answer by writing their answers in the stream so that you can answer in real time.

6. **Learn from your replays.** Periscope keeps your broadcast on their app for 24 hours allowing people (and you) to look at it again and/or to share it with their own followers. Which parts of the broadcast saw the best engagements? When did you lose viewers?

In August 2015 Facebook decided to jump on the live-streaming bandwagon and introduced Facebook "Live" as a feature in its Mentions app. Never heard of Mentions? Don't worry, most people haven't. Mentions is used, according to Facebook, by 200,000 professionals with verified profiles to manage their online presence. It allows them to create alerts on their company name, brand and/or competitors and so much more. This includes Live-streaming, but you do need to be a verified profile in order to have access.

Facebook Live gives public figures a Facebook equivalent of Periscope, and the functionality is very similar. The popularity of other live streaming apps makes it likely that Facebook will expand Mentions access to the wider public eventually. Once it does, the competition will get very interesting.

Facebook Mentions, Periscope and Meerkat.

Snapchat

Snapchat is an app that allows people to send each other photos and videos that disappear after ten seconds. This decay feature gave Snapchat a huge advantage early on, and it became the default option for people who wanted to send each other 'sexts' or content that they didn't want to be recorded anywhere. Third party apps like Quick Save and SnapSave Free started appearing, which allowed people to save their messages, and after it emerged that Snapchat retains all messages, some of the perceived security advantages lost a bit of weight. Snapchat then released a 'Replay' feature that allows you to replay 3 messages, once, for 0.99¢.

Snapchat's core audience is between 13 and 25 years old and 70% of its users are women. On an average day, these guys are sending approximately 400 million snaps. This all proved too good to miss for brands that want to target this audience, and various large companies have been exploring its viability as an Ad platform. Taco Bell used Snapchat to promote the re-release of the Beefy Crunch Burrito and asked users to follow them in exchange for a secret snap of the release date of their burrito. This type of campaign makes the most of the secret and personal feeling of receiving a snap, and Taco Bell's 200,000 have a high level of engagement (it's estimated that 80% of these followers open their snaps) because their social media team comes across *real* (and uses tons of emojis). Teen fashion retailer Wet Seal handed its account over to a 16-year-old blogger for a couple of days, resulting in 9,000 new followers and 6,000 views of the "My Story".

For businesses targeting the teenage audience, Snapchat is an interesting channel. Here are four ways of getting the most out of Snapchat for your business:

1. **Do your research.** The obvious first question is should your brand be on Snapchat? If your customers use Snapchat frequently, that tells you that it's worth testing. If they don't, it's one to keep on your radar but with so many channels out there it might not be the best use

of your time at the moment. If your audience is the 13 to 25 year old age group, it's definitely worth testing. Some larger corporations including CNN, Food Network and some car companies like Acura have an active presence on Snapchat, appealing to both young and old audiences with varying degrees of success.

2. **Decide what you want out of your Snapchat.** Will you be focusing on contests, new product sneak peeks, coupons, behind the scenes, new team member introductions and/or targeting videos?

3. **Remind your social audience.** Keep reminding your audience on more established channels like Facebook, Instagram, and Twitter that you're on Snapchat and doing things there that they won't see unless they follow you.

4. **Post frequently.** If you want to stay on people's radars, set a regular schedule and stick to it.

If you're contemplating a push on Snapchat, it's important that the tone you present is as close as possible to the tone your audience uses with each other. CNN, for example, are trying to capture a younger audience than their regular viewers (who are typically NOT 13 year old girls). Their strategy is to adopt a more playful tone than it does on other social networks:

TECH 02 ⊙

TOO SMART FOR OUR OWN GOOD?

Tech and science experts say we need to ban "killer robots" – or artificially intelligent weapons – because they could be dangerous for humanity.

In the end, it's all about creating a balance between keeping true to your brand message while also appealing to the core audience of Snapchat.

The Nitty Gritty: Social Media Tools

So you've created all your social media accounts, planned a starting strategy, and are ready to start posting. The good news is that there are plenty of tools out there to help you manage the posting, interaction and analysis of your social campaigns. Let's look at two of the most popular ones, Buffer and Hootsuite.

Hootsuite

Hootsuite allows you to manage multiple social media accounts across different platforms. It is one of the most popular free social media management tools with good reason. It integrates with all of the most popular networks, including Instagram, allowing you to block out some time to spend creating posts and have Hootsuite post these at a schedule you decide.

Pros:
- It comes with free, pro, and enterprise licensing options so the fee scales as your campaign does.
- You can use it to manage Twitter, Instagram, Facebook, LinkedIn, WordPress, Google Plus, and Foursquare.

- It offers a useful monitoring service that shows you replies, mentions and direct messages from all networks in one dashboard.
- It has the ability to schedule updates (Tweets, Facebook posts), including posting across all your networks at a set time.
- Collaboration options allow you to work as a team and delegate replies and other tasks with staff.
- It provides very insightful and customised analytics, good enough to present to management or clients without much additional work.
- It has good mobile apps for Android, iOS, and BlackBerry.

Cons:
- Although the app is marketed as free, the features in the free version are quite limited.
- The analytics features aren't available in the free version. Detailed analytics can be expensive - as low as $50 and as high as $500 per report.
- You are restricted to the ow.ly URL shortener. For most this isn't a problem, but if you have your own short URL or use another service for the analytics, Hootsuite probably isn't for you.
- The collaborative teams feature, while very neat, is relatively expensive.

The Verdict? Social media monitoring is something that Hootsuite does well, because it allows you to create custom streams to show all Tweets including a particular keyword, phrase, Hashtag, mention or list. Hootsuite is a good 'getting started' tool for small businesses that don't necessarily have a budget to pay for something more advanced, but need some help keeping on top of all their networks.

The Pro upgraded version starts at less than $10/month and gives you more options, including more social profiles, bulk message scheduling, some reporting and access to premium Apps.

Buffer

Buffer's free version is less useful than the free version of Hootsuite. Not only does it limit the number of accounts you can link, but also the number of updates you can post. The paid version is very good, however:

Pros
- With one easy click you'll be able to share content and schedule posts via Twitter, Facebook, LinkedIn, Google+ and Pinterest.
- Buffer also allows you to share and schedule on Pinterest however it is through another app called Tailwind, which is a paid application ($9.99 per month). Buffer has integrated pinning into its platform on their paid plans.

- Buffer has Pablo, a free image creation tool that can help you create social media images for Facebook, Twitter, Pinterest and Google+ very quickly.
- Lets you select your default shortener as the well-known bit.ly, and also offers buff.ly and j.mp.
- The buffer extension for Chrome is also a helpful addition (Hootsuite also has their own extension called the Hootlet). The extension allows you share links, pictures and videos from wherever you are on the web. The extension also allows you to choose the single composer option or power scheduler where you can post the same thing multiple times over a specific period of time.
- Buffer analytics is useful, showing your best and worst performing posts based on engagement (which you can filter by engagement type, i.e. Retweets, favourites, replies, likes, comments, clicks), reach, and post type (image posts, link posts, text posts and your Retweets). All of this is exportable too, if you need to do any further analysis.
- It'll help you find the best times to post, and automatically time your posts to get maximum engagement.
- Clean and simple layout.
- You can integrate blog feeds to give you sources of content to post out.

- Paid plans cost from only USD$10/month

Cons
- No Instagram integration into the platform
- No monitoring tools for mentions, searches and Hashtags, so you'll have to monitor these from another tool or through the networks themselves.

The Verdict? If you're looking for a social media management platform, then Buffer isn't for you. It's not that Buffer isn't an amazing tool, but its primary use is publishing and scheduling content. The Awesome Plan is USD$10 a month and offers: up to 10 social profiles, 100 posts in your Buffer, varied schedules and 15 RSS feeds per connected profile. If you need more options, such as adding more social profiles or adding team members, Buffer also has three different types of paid business options ranging from USD$50 to USD$250 /month depending on your needs.

Whilst Buffer and Hootsuite are the two most popular social media tools, there are many others. The best of the rest include:

Tweetdeck: Another free tool that allows you to manage Twitter more effectively. You can organise and build custom timelines, keep track of lists, searches, activity and more - all on one interface and all for free. It allows you to schedule Tweets to be posted in the future, and lets you filter searches based on criteria like engagement, users and content type. For example you can add a stream that shows anyone who has Tweeted #iloveLondon. One of the best features about Tweetdeck is the ability to bypass Twitter's famous 140 characters limit. You can type a longer Tweet and Tweetdeck will automatically shorten it up for you, creating a link that, when clicked, will lead the reader to a page containing the full Tweet. Some say this defeats the point of Twitter, but for those occasions where you absolutely positively have to use more characters it's an absolute lifesaver!

Trello: Trello is a project management tool that you might find useful if you need to coordinate the team working on your social campaign. In one glance, Trello tells you what's being worked on, who's working on it, and where something is in a process.

Sprout Social: A paid social media management tool that can manage, post, monitor, and analyse multiple social media accounts from one place, Sprout Social offers similar functionality to Hootsuite, although with plans starting from $59, it's a little more expensive.

Sprinklr: Sprinklr is an enterprise-grade social media and website management platform that combines all your marketing channels in one dashboard. Priced out of the reach of most SMEs, it costs USD$50,000 upwards but offers a level of automation beyond any its more affordable competitors.

IFTTT: IFTTT (standing for If This, Then That) is an automation tool that allows you to trigger actions based on particular events. For example *if this* [publish a new article on your blog] *than that* [Tweet a link to the new article]. Best of all, it works well with Buffer and Hootsuite. The possibilities are limited only by how creative you can be, whether posting to Facebook by leaving a speech-to-text voicemail, or emailing people to thank them for following you on Twitter.

Canva: To create beautiful pictures, you can either get good at using Photoshop, or check out Canva. Its simple interface allows you to easily create beautiful designs Infographics with no technical ability, just by dragging and dropping each element. Use a bunch of preloaded images, or pick your own. It's also free, making it a total win.

Tailwind: A paid Pinterest management tool, Tailwind allows you to create an optimal pin schedule, schedule multiple pins at a time, schedule reminders and monitor a handy set of analytics data.

Whichever you opt for, social media management tools *do* make a lot of sense, particularly for the scheduling functionality. Keeping your feed topped up and monitoring interactions can become very time consuming and a constant distraction without setting aside time each day to use a tool like Buffer. Whether for your sanity or your time, we encourage you to try out the options and see which suits you best.

Google Plus

So what about Google+? In June 2011, Google unveiled its social media platform, Google Plus. Many of us were somewhat skeptical about the need for yet another social media platform, but for Google the advertising opportunity that social media presents is just too important to ignore. It had to do *something*, and Google+ was the result. But it never really took off in the way they hoped. Low engagement levels amongst individuals meant that it remained a ghost town for businesses until November 2015, when Google finally broke off the business functionality (local map listings, reviews etc.) and the rest of Google+. At the time of writing, it is unclear what the future holds for these local listings, but Google+ itself has transitioned to a community tool rather than anything that holds significance for those of us looking to generate traffic to our businesses.

Listening

Although much of the time spent on social media marketing focuses on *talking* and pushing out your message (because that is what drives your audience), listening has a really important role to play too. The opportunity to listen to existing conversations going on around the world is one of the most exciting aspects, and very few take full advantage. Those that do often limit their listening to mentions of their brand or company name which, if they are a small or medium-sized business, are few and far between.

In this section we're going to explore listening at a deeper level. We'll explore its use as a method of attracting new customers and generating leads through a process we call Outbound Social Lead Generation (OSLG) and show how you can directly profit from your competitor's mistakes (and lack of listening!)

The approach that is talked about in many social media marketing books and courses is naturally suited to large companies that already attract a lot of social media discussion. They advise to listen out for mentions of your brand name, and try to settle any public customer service disputes quickly. Great (if obvious) advice, but what does the local cake shop, plumber or accountant do when they only get a few mentions per week — or less — on Twitter, and mostly from people they already know?

The truth is that listening out for mentions of your own business is only the starting point. In this chapter we'll be exploring how those businesses that aren't yet receiving a lot of inbound Tweets and Facebook posts can use existing conversations to grow their customer base.

Customer Service & Handling Complaints

If you have large, established competitors who receive complaints via social media and don't respond quickly or effectively, there's nothing to stop YOU from dealing with those complaints on their behalf. Disgruntled customers who feel ignored on social are ripe for poaching, so any negative mentions of your competitors can be met with a sensitive apology on their behalf and a link to a free trial of your service instead. Your goal with this sort of interaction is to introduce yourself then immediately take the discussion private to continue the sale.

Dealing With Public Complaints

If you get some of your own complaints (and as you grow, you will), your first goal is to show that you've listened. Acknowledging the complainer and offering to investigate further with them through direct message or over the phone shows them that you're committed to fixing the issue.

Taking things private serves three main purposes:

1. It removes the complainer's soapbox. Taking away their audience also diffuses the complainant's power, and they'll often respond to this power play by doing absolutely nothing; the complaint dies there and then (although the dissatisfaction lingers...). You'll see brands Tweet things like "@Timninjakitchen I am sorry to hear that. If you can DM us your account number we'll get this looking into for you." Some will, many won't be bothered.

2. The privacy allows sharing of sensitive customer information so the problem can be addressed properly.

3. It puts the onus on the complainant. *They* now have to act. Whether it's following the brand and sending a direct message with customer service numbers or transaction IDs, this requires more effort than simply writing a Tweet moaning about a perceived injustice. For many complaints, this effort is too much and the complaint diffuses there and then.

Stay strong but don't be aggressive

Although it's not a good idea to *avoid* apologising or admitting fault, it's important that your brand keeps its integrity. Publicly commenting on particular cases or mentioning specific team members is generally unnecessary and has the potential to damage your reputation, as well as the morale of any team members mentioned. Like the martial arts principle of Jū, you want to accept your opponent's attack and use it to your advantage rather than stand rigidly and take a punch to the face. So instead of dwelling on the problem or getting too caught up in apportioning blame, focus on finding a solution that makes everyone happy.

Showing aggression or defiance in complaint responses is a recipe for disaster, and things can quickly get out of hand. In a recent episode of TV show Kitchen Nightmares featuring fiery chef Gordon Ramsay, an Arizona restaurant called Amy's Baking Company failed to capitalise on the good publicity a nationwide TV appearance *should* have caused, and instead began one of the most terrifying (yet entertaining) social media meltdowns in history.

Their Facebook page (https://www.facebook.com/amysbakingco) was targeted by viewers who started leaving comments about the show and the owner Amy. Amy and the team responded with aggression, which in turn attracted more attention. As the page began to go viral on social sharing site Reddit, more and more people began leaving comments not just about the show and staff, but how they were handling the rapidly accelerating runaway train. This in turn produced even more aggressive responses from the page owners who by now had started a full-scale meltdown:

"I AM WONDER WOMAN. I AM A GREAT CHEF, A GREAT WIFE, AND A GREAT MOM TO MY KIDS. AND WE WILL BE PARENTS TO A HUMAN KID, ONE DAY TO. WE WILL SHOW ALL OF YOU."

"WE ARE NOT FREAKING OUT. WE DO NOT CARE ABOUT A "WITCH HUNT" I AM NOT A WITCH. I AM GODS CHILD. P*** OFF ALL OF YOU. F*** REDDITS, F*** YELP AND F*** ALL OF YOU. BRING IT. WE WILL FIGHT BACK."

Nothing says 'calm and controlled' like caps lock, right? For those who enjoy that sort of thing, the Facebook page is well worth a visit.

Clearly this is an extreme example, but cases like this prove that meeting hostility with aggression just doesn't work online. Once situations get emotional they have the potential to quickly get out of control. Social communities gather like sharks as soon as they detect blood in the water. The takeaway is no matter how personal the issue feels, try to never respond in an emotional way.

Almost every business will, at some point, have dissatisfied customers. Some people just don't *want* to be happy and it doesn't matter what you do, they will stubbornly refuse. It's just part of doing business and a side effect of serving a lot of people. When the comments come, it's important to learn from them and meet them in a respectful and appreciative way on social.

Measuring Influence

The truth is that not all of your followers and fans are equally important to you. Endorsement from your most influential followers can be worth a lot more to your bottom line than happy Tweets from a regular Joe. These influencers tend to have a larger audience and more power over that audience. If you can turn them into raving fans for your business, they'll do the promotion for you. But how can you identify who in your audience is most influential?

Klout (www.klout.com) aims to bring the measurement of influence to social media. Your Klout score is a number from 1 - 100 based on your relationship with your followers, the engagement of your updates and the topics on which you are considered an influencer. For example, if you regularly Tweet out content that gets shared, replied to and favourited, your Klout score will be higher than someone who's Tweets get no reaction. If your Facebook posts get a lot of likes, comments and shares, you'll have more Klout than someone with few friends who rarely uses it. Klout measures and combines influence on each of your social networks to give you one overall score.

While a single algorithm might not be able to measure influence 100% accurately, Klout is a pretty good indicator and does a neat job of representing something so complex in a single number. The Klout plugin for Google's Chrome browser displays Twitter users' Klout scores next to their profile pictures when you use the Twitter web interface, which is really useful when you're browsing, checking @replies and doing outreach to influential people in your market.

With this indication of influence you'll be able to prioritise your time and energy on the most important contacts and those with the potential to spread your message furthest.

Of course all this talk of prioritising influential people doesn't mean that you should neglect those with low Klout scores or treat your less influential followers like irrelevant outcasts; they might simply have not set up their Klout account properly or be in the habit of creating shareworthy content yet. Today's low Klout scorers might be tomorrow's influencers, so relationships that you make with them now could lead to much greater exposure for you in the future. It really depends how much time and energy you have to dedicate to your social outreach, and Klout score is just one more metric for helping you make informed decisions.

Social Media For Lead Generation

The potential for using social media to bring you highly qualified fresh leads is really exciting. What's more, unlike forms of advertising where a potential customer has to actively search for a solution to their problem in order to be shown an ad, social media gives you the ability to reach out to people who are complaining and present a solution, *without them having to do any of the work*. We can be right there at the point of pain, offering a targeted solution.

In the sections covering advertising we look at targeting people according to *their likes and interests*, but the strategies we're covering in this section are even more focused and can bring an unbelievable response rate. They involve a little more work than set-and-forget adverts, but with the right offer and sales process they can be extremely profitable.

OSLG (Outbound Social Lead Generation)

OSLG is particularly exciting for businesses that solve a problem, particularly in a local market. Because it's new, this sort of strategy is very unlikely to be on your competitors' radars. People tend to spend money on advertising that is sold by someone, whether it's local newspapers, Yellow Pages (remember that?) or Google Adwords. OSLG isn't sold by anyone on a large scale (yet), so it's just not part of their consciousness.

The principle of Outbound Social Lead Generation is this: people are in your area complaining about problems that your product or service solves. By offer help, advice or a targeted offer over social media, you can be in their consciousness right at the point when they need you most. For example:

"They say it comes in 3's first a broken dryer then my boiler packed up again now a burst water pipe in my bathroom! #VERYANNOYED" @Suzie (Twitter handle disguised)

This Tweet got no responses from plumbers, despite the fact that there are plenty of them in Suzie's city, and many are paying an average £2.30 per click on Google Adwords to reach people with plumbing problems. Here is a potential customer crying for help and no one came to the rescue.

Searching for locally relevant Tweets used to require third party apps and plenty of hassle, but it's now easier than ever thanks to Twitter's own advanced search. In the example above, all any of the plumbers in Newcastle upon Tyne would have to do is search for:

boiler near:"Newcastle upon tyne" within:10mi

This tells Twitter to find Tweets using the word 'boiler' within 10 miles of Newcastle-upon-Tyne. It's simple and if they're monitoring this search they'll be seeing jobs pop up that their competitors would have no idea about.
While they might not be getting three jobs per day from this strategy, it's free and can be set up to take no time at all.

But perhaps the plumber doesn't only want to find boiler jobs?

boiler OR plumber OR drainage OR blocked drain OR central heating OR radiator near:"Newcastle upon tyne" within:10mi

If they want to get really fancy and narrow the search to Tweets that have negative intent and include a question, they can search:

boiler OR plumber OR drainage OR blocked drain OR central heating OR radiator near:"Newcastle upon tyne" within:10mi :(?

And so on. The list of Twitter search operators is extensive (see below) and how you use them will depend on your specific market and your audience.

Once you've identified a search that works for your market and brings up relevant Tweets, you can save it. This allows you to access it quickly in future from a Twitter app on your computer or phone. Using an application like Tweetdeck can give you the option to keep this search open at all times, seeing live updates as new Tweets come in.

Operator	Finds Tweets...
Twitter search	containing both "twitter" and "search". This is the default operator.
"happy hour"	containing the exact phrase "happy hour".
love OR hate	containing either "love" or "hate" (or both).
beer -root	containing "beer" but not "root".
#haiku	containing the hashtag "haiku".
from:alexiskold	sent from person "alexiskold".
to:techcrunch	sent to person "techcrunch".
@mashable	referencing person "mashable".
"happy hour" near:"san	containing the exact phrase "happy

francisco"	hour" and sent near "san francisco".
near:NYC within:15mi	sent within 15 miles of "NYC".
superhero since:2010-12-27	containing "superhero" and sent since date "2010-12-27" (year-month-day).
ftw until:2010-12-27	containing "ftw" and sent up to date "2010-12-27".
movie -scary :)	containing "movie", but not "scary", and with a positive attitude.
flight :(	containing "flight" and with a negative attitude.
traffic ?	containing "traffic" and asking a question.
hilarious filter:links	containing "hilarious" and linking to URLs.
news source:twitterfeed	containing "news" and entered via TwitterFeed

Twitter search operators. Source: twitter.com

Alerts can be configured meaning that you find out as soon as someone posts a Tweet matching your criteria.

If you want to identify your own OSLG target customer, here are some questions to ask:

- How might you identify people who are in need of your product or service?

- Do they buy something else around the same time that they need you? For example personal trainers can strike when the iron is hot by congratulating and offering tips to those Tweeting about joining a gym or checking in for the first time.
- Are your customers at a certain place in life when they need your service? For example local furniture stores could send Tweets welcoming people to the area and offering a 'welcome free gift' if they Tweet or post updates about moving into a new house or apartment and are located within 10 miles. Wedding venues can send congratulatory Tweets to people within a 40-mile radius posting statuses, Tweets or pictures about getting engaged. As can wedding photographers, catering companies, wedding planners etc. All of these service categories will, at some point, be required by the Tweeter, so how better to introduce yourself than offer a simple congratulations and a free gift? It's still so unusual that you are very likely to get noticed.

This part requires your creativity as well as a little experimentation, both in your targeting and your approach. As clichéd as it is, 'thinking outside the box' here can really help position you in a completely different way to your competitors, who are stuck standing in their shops hoping and praying that someone walks in needing what they offer.

Making the Sale

It's one thing to see Tweets from people complaining about a problem that you can solve, but how do you make the sale?

The important thing to remember is that the person Tweeting was not asking for business solicitations, nor are they expecting it. By bursting in and immediately pitching your service you're not going to be making friends *or* sales. As with all social media marketing, the best approach is to offer value first. Just letting someone in distress know that you've heard their cry and are here to help them if they need you is a good first step to building rapport.

If you're able to offer some specific advice that could help them partially (or even completely) solve their problem, you should take that opportunity as well. Remember your goal for social media is to build long-term awareness and create a community of potential customers who understand your value and consider you an authority. Even if that means offering advice to someone rather than straight up pitching them, you should take that opportunity because of what it could lead to in future.

If a helpful and polite plumber replied to @Suzie above giving some tips for stopping the water leak, limiting damage to her bathroom and offering to come and take a look immediately free of charge, that's going to be a tough series of Tweets to ignore. If the tone is helpful and sympathetic rather than coming across like a shark smelling blood, the potential customer's first impression of the plumber is of someone who wants to help.

By taking the time out of their day and offering value (the tips) the plumber is demonstrating a willingness to help beyond just pitching their service. If @Suzie has already found someone to fix the solution, the Twitter plumber is still providing useful advice (how to limit damage) and @Suzie is likely to say thank you, at which point the plumber says "not to worry, if you need any help in future just Tweet us!" and clicks to follow her. @Suzie likes the sound of this help, feels a duty to reciprocate the kind Tweets and the follow so decides to follow the plumber back. Target engaged.

@Suzie is now in the plumber's herd and by providing *interesting* and *useful* Tweets in future (not things like "Watching the football" or "Stuck in traffic today") the plumber can begin to establish himself on Suzie's radar. Next time there's a leak, who is @Suzie going to call (or Tweet)?

As well as offering original content to help someone, you can also direct him or her to other content on the net that solves his or her problem. While sending them somewhere else might initially seem counterintuitive, it actually positions you as a knowledgeable expert who thinks beyond their own gain, and just wants to help.

If your potential customers tend to face a similar set of problems, you can put together a quick FAQ section on your website. Then, next time someone complains about-facing one of these problems, a simple message offering sympathy and a link to the page containing the solution is all you need to position yourself and begin the relationship.

As you can see, Outbound Social Lead Generation is miles away from what most businesses are using social media for. This makes resistance extremely low amongst targets of such a campaign, as they are not yet tuning this sort of social outreach out. Your advertising can fly under their radar, because after all — if it looks like a friendly Tweet and smells like a friendly Tweet, it must just be a friendly Tweet, right?

Straightforward Business Solicitations

While in my searches, I came across the following Tweet which illustrates perfectly the type of situation where a business needs to pitch their offering in one Tweet:

Please can anybody recommend a #plumber in the #lichfield area as #boiler has packed up @thisisLichfield @LichfieldLive @LichfieldBlog

Someone please sell this guy some plumbing! How might you approach this sort of situation?

Time is of the essence here. You need to be the first on the scene with a compelling Tweet and a strong call to action in order to get your foot in the door before anybody else. Although this Tweeter is looking for someone to fix their boiler, what they're really asking for is recommendations. This shows that social proof and personal recommendation are important to them, and can be considered one of their primary sales triggers.

Armed with information about the problem and a clear idea for how they make buying decisions, you can create a well-crafted proposition that matches them closely. It has to be brief to fit in Twitter's 140-character limit, so there's no room for messing around. The format should be:

- Clear relevant benefit
- Strong call to action

In this case a clear relevant benefit could be the number of personal recommendations: "95% of our customers refer us to friends", "we're the most shared plumber in your town", or even just "most of our work comes from word-of-mouth". If actual Twitter users can be included in the Tweet ("@tony called about our emergency boiler repair "best service from a plumber ever"), so much the better. If you need more space, consider using one Tweet for the benefit statement and one for the follow-up call to action.

For the call to action, we want to be strong and compelling but also offer something low risk and relatively low commitment. "Call us now" is NEVER a strong enough call to action on its own, because it doesn't answer any of the customer's questions, and leaves a considerable amount of doubt about what will happen next. Offer something that is difficult to turn down, whether it's a free gift for enquiring, free no obligation inspection or something else that involves very little risk for them with a large potential reward.

In the specific case above, my recommendation would be to offer a free inspection and prescription for the repair. It should be emphasised that this inspection comes with no obligation, and no hard sales pitch will be made (though of course a clear explanation of the problem and the cost to fix the problem will be outlined, and at that point the job is likely to be agreed).

If offering some sort of low commitment offer on the front end isn't viable, consider offer a new customer discount or free gift with first purchase in order to motivate people to act. If your profit-per-transaction is high, or your customers have a high 'lifetime value' then you can obviously afford to do more than a business with a very low cost-per-transaction or who sells one-off or infrequent purchases.

Knowing what you can afford to spend to attract each new lead requires that you understand some of your business's fundamental numbers:

- How much you are willing to spend to attract each new customer. If your average transaction size generates £100 profit, you might decide you are willing to spend £50 to generate each new sale.
- What your conversion rate is from leads to customers. For example if you know that on average one in every three new leads ends up buying from you, your conversion rate is ⅓ or 33%. You then know that you'll need to bring in three new leads each time you want one new customer
- Cost per lead. This is how much you can spend on each lead. If you are willing to spend £50 on acquiring a new customer and you convert one in three leads, you now know that you can spend £50/3 = £16.66 on attracting each lead.

A free £15 shopping voucher just for enquiring is viable under these conditions.

Of course, the more tempting you make your 'bait' or free gift, the more unqualified leads you might attract, so it's important to keep re-evaluating your cost per lead and cost per customer.

Capitalising On Your Competitors' Mistakes

Because of the amount of social media marketing incompetence out there, capitalising on the mistakes of others in your industry can offer some easy pickings. Luckily people *love* to complain on social media. When we've had a bad experience with a particular company, complaining in public can feel extremely satisfying as our voice is finally being heard. We've covered how to deal with this for your own business elsewhere, but in this section we'll look at some different approaches you can take to capitalise on your competitors' inability to deal with customer complaints.

This strategy can work particularly well for businesses that pride themselves on offering a higher level of customer service than more established competitors, but really any business can take advantage of their rivals' inability to keep all of their customers happy.

In order to be there just at the right moment, you'll want to monitor mentions of your competitors and any relevant brand or product names. Each time somebody mentions that they're having a problem with your competitor, you send a sympathetic Tweet or post apologising for the problem. That's it — you don't need to pitch them or explain why your service is better. Remember the reason most people vent their anger on social media is because they want to feel that they're being *listened to* and that the company responsible has recognised their problem. Sometimes a solution isn't possible or practical, but just the fact that they have had their complaint heard is enough to improve their mood. They are not necessarily in the right frame of mind to be pitched at, and might not be in a position to buy, so pitching your service is unnecessary and changes the vibe of your message from 'nice' to 'advert'.

But your offer of sympathy puts you on their radar. If they *are* unhappy and ready to buy, then you are there right when they need you and you've differentiated yourself from the others in your market by showing that you care. They can investigate further and will be intrigued to see why you've responded to their Tweet when often the company they are moaning about hasn't. They'll likely check your profile, your other recent Tweets (to see if you do this sort of thing a lot), and will visit your website if it's linked from your profile.

Clearly, the more influential the complainant, the more effective this strategy can be at generating shares, RTs and other coverage.

Demonstrating your Expertise

Many businesses underestimate the value of the expertise contained within their team. Even if you are relatively new in your field, the fact that you spend your time specialising in something gives you expertise over and above your customers.

Say for example you're a hair stylist working straight out of college; there are dozens/hundreds/thousands of potential clients in your area who would appreciate an honest opinion on what sort of hairstyle might suit them. If you're a wedding photographer, offering five tips to judge a good wedding photographer from a bad one would be extremely useful for the hundreds of brides and grooms nearby who pay for wedding photography each year without really knowing what they should be looking for.

What sort of expertise is present in your business, and who would benefit from it? Just like the other listening strategies we've discussed, demonstrating your expertise is a great opportunity to put yourself in front of people who have identified themselves as potential future customers and position yourself as an authority who cares.

Whether you create a formalised process for demonstrating your expertise (offering audits, quotes or consultations) or you just get into the habit of answering questions people write you on your blog or through social media, being able to demonstrate your expertise in public can give you a real 'authority' persona on social media. Holding Q&A sessions, Google+ hangouts, writing and promoting blog posts that answer some of the most common questions or making videos explaining your answers can all lead to shares, RTs and wider publicity in your industry. Of course, none of this happens overnight and it requires a level of commitment, especially in the early days when there will be more As than Qs.

Measuring Social Media ROI

In the world of social media, many marketing companies view ROI (return on investment) as a bit of a dirty word. It's as if Pope Julius II was stood in the Sistine Chapel yelling up at Michelangelo asking the ROI on his ceiling painting, and demanding to see projections of the increased tourist donations he could expect in the centuries to follow. But fine art social media isn't, and we believe it should be a business decision made just like any other — cost in vs. profit out. Just because it has a bit of a soft and fluffy image doesn't mean it's not useful in a hard-nosed business sense as well, as long as proper tracking is put in place.

It's true that there are a lot of untrackable benefits to social media. As an extension of word of mouth, the sort of brand awareness and familiarity that a good social media campaign can generate — not to mention individual customer service queries — can not always be quantified. But that doesn't prevent us from being fastidious about collecting data and measuring the effects of our work on traffic and sales as much as we can.

At the risk of sounding contradictory, we recommend almost *every single client* who gets in touch wanting to improve their website ranking starts using social media if they're not already; not because it will directly lead to sales for them, but because the SEO benefits are usually enough *on their own* to warrant an active campaign.

Different Tracking Scenarios

How you track your social media ROI will depend heavily on your website's purpose and overall marketing plan. A pure e-commerce site will clearly require different tracking to a roofer who wants to generate phone calls, whilst a local business relying on in-person visits has their own set of tracking challenges altogether.

In the following section we'll go through different tracking techniques so you can pick and choose those that suit your particular business and match your technical capabilities.

First Touch vs Last Touch

One final point before we dive in is understanding the importance of a complete marketing funnel and where each of your marketing pieces (including social media) fits in. In tracking, the concepts of 'first touch' (the first time the user comes across your brand or a product) and 'last touch' (the final step that leads them to buy) are useful to understand the role that a variety of different pieces of the puzzle have, to make sure we're not over-crediting or under-crediting any single marketing piece. To illustrate, let's take an example:

Some of the readers of this book will claim the free website and marketing review from www.profitablesocialmediamarketing.com. They'll go to the website, fill in the form and receive a detailed audit with suggestions on how to boost their own social media profile and use it to grow their business. Once they've received this audit, many of them will ask us to implement this social media campaign for them. Some of them will talk to us on the phone, some will use email.

So which piece of this marketing puzzle (the book, the website, the audit, phone conversation or the email follow up) do we attribute the sale to? For sure nothing would have happened without the book (first touch), but likewise without the phone conversation or email follow up (last touch) the sale wouldn't have happened either. To make matters even more complicated, some of the readers of this book will have found us through referrals from other clients, social media, one of our other books, YouTube, footer links in websites that are outperforming theirs, magazine articles, interviews and so on. All this could happen before they even join the 'book - website - audit - follow-up - sale' path.

So while we can track either first touch (leads generated by social media) or last touch (sales/conversions directly resulting from social media messages) for your social media marketing campaign, it's important not to get too caught up in expecting each Tweet to result in X sales or worrying that you only have 300 followers, and instead look at the big picture and combination of *all* your online marketing efforts.

Google Analytics for Social Media

Google Analytics gives us some fantastic measuring tools for social media, mostly around clicks, visitors and traffic. You can use it to see how many visitors are coming into your site from each network, how long they are staying, what they are reading while they are there and how many of them turn into customers, leads or other conversions. While an exhaustive explanation of all the features, uses and analysis available in Google Analytics is beyond the scope of this book, we'll take a look at the social media dashboard inside Google Analytics and understand some of the most useful social media specific features. If you're interested in learning more about Google Analytics, we have a free tutorial series at www.exposureninja.com/google-analytics

If you don't already have Google Analytics set up and installed on your website, head over to www.google.com/analytics and sign up. Once you've filled in your website's details you'll be given a piece of code which you or your website ninja will need to add to each page that you want to track (basically all of them, minus any 'hidden' pages). There's plenty of help available to set up Google Analytics online, and Google's own documentation is pretty good if you get stuck.

Once you've got Analytics up and running and you're starting to see some stats, like where your visitors are arriving on your site from (in the Traffic Sources section) we're ready to start getting a little more involved with the social aspect and setting up some **goals**.

Google Analytics goals are used to give an easily defined result that we can use to measure the effectiveness of the promotion we do for your website. A goal can be many different things; signups, contact form submissions, clicking 'more' to see more information, a product purchase on an e-commerce website, playing a video, viewing contact information or becoming an affiliate. By defining and measuring these goals, not only can you track how effective your social media campaign is, you'll also be able to compare its effectiveness to other sources of traffic such as Google ads, organic search and direct traffic. This data can show you the *value* of your social media traffic. You might find that your traffic from Pinterest is a low percentage of all the visitors on your site but that these visitors tend to be better buyers than visitors from

317

organic Google searches. Or vice versa. Whatever patterns you find, having the *data* means you can make informed decisions about where to focus your promotion.

Setting Up a Goal

To set up a goal for your site, go to Admin in your Analytics dashboard, and click Goals. You'll see a button to set up a New Goal that will take you through the process of defining your goals. You can select a template from a list of sample goals, write a description and choose what sort of action defines the goal, for example landing on a thank you page after filling in a form or requesting more information. You can then define the goal in specific terms, for example choosing a destination URL that people visit once they have filled in a form on your site. You can also assign it a monetary value (if, for example, you know your average value per lead) as well as define any funnel that you have to lead people through the process of filling in the form or placing an order.

It's as simple as that! Once your goal is set up you can choose to verify it if you want to make sure it's 'wired up' properly, and then you're ready to start collecting data.

Because social media tends to generate links and traffic in a slightly different way to regular 'static' links, there is a special Social section inside the Google Analytics dashboard. Go to Traffic Sources / Social / Overview to get started. If you've set up a monetary value on your goals, this dashboard will show an estimate of you how much your social media traffic has been worth to you, broken down by Conversions, Contributed Social Conversions (conversions where social played a role anywhere along the path) and Last Interaction Social Conversions (conversions where social media was the 'last touch' sending the visitor to the site to buy).

You'll also be able to see the stats for each social network, helping you to identify which networks bring the most traffic as a percentage of total social traffic. The Network Referrals tab gives more information about this, including how many pages visitors from each network visit on your site, as well as how long they stay. This can be quite an instructive statistic as it gives a glimpse into the relative quality of traffic from each network. These stats will be different according to your market and the content promoted on each network.

For example one of our clients in home maintenance gets a small amount of traffic from video sites like YouTube and Dailymotion as a result of some promotional videos we made for them. While this traffic doesn't make up a large percentage of his *overall* traffic (organic search is by far the largest referrer),

319

visitors from these video sites *are* extremely engaged, with their visits lasting an average of around six times as long as those who arrive from organic search. This tells us that for this particular service, video is an incredibly powerful tool. Those visitors who find the site through YouTube or Dailymotion (often through organic Google searches where they see these videos showing up in the search results) view on average between two and six times more pages per visit than those visitors who land on the site having seen something on Tumblr, Stumbleupon or Wordpress.

If your site suddenly starts getting an increase in traffic from social, checking the Landing Pages tab can help you to identify the content that is being shared, and on which social networks so you can focus more attention on promoting it. What we'll often see is that particular social networks respond well to certain types of content. According to a July 2013 study by Gigya, Pinterest is responsible for 41% of all e-commerce traffic generated by social media, compared to 16% of all traffic overall. If you own an e-commerce website that gets a good amount of image shares of your products on Pinterest, this will come as no surprise to you. Neither will the fact that Pinterest traffic tends to convert at higher rates and spend more.

Using breakdowns of social traffic by page or by social network can really help you hone your social media

320

campaign and put more resources into the sources already shown to be working and bringing you in leads.

Your Social Media Plan

In this final section, we'll be piecing together everything discussed above and helping you to create your perfect* social media campaign.

*There's a saying that goes: "great books aren't written they're *rewritten*" (ahem). Likewise the perfect social media campaign isn't designed in one go, but honed over time as a result of testing, tweaking and retesting. Recognise that if you're new to social media there will almost certainly be a significant period of trial and error before you find the formula and approach that works best for you. In this sense then, the perfect social media campaign is built around refocus, testing and measuring results.

Your Social Media campaign needs to begin with a plan of action identifying the three key marketing elements discussed at the start of this book:

1. Your **M**essage
2. Your **M**arket
3. Your **M**ethod of communication

Your message is the basis of all that follows. It's the online identity that your company adopts and it shapes every piece of content that you publish.

The first step is to identify the goal or goals of your social media campaign from the following:

1. Social Selling
2. Loyalty & Retention
3. Rising Awareness

Once you've got your goal specific, you need to think about the personality of the social profile. Remember that different personalities will appeal to different markets, and your social profile will essentially be the personification of your brand. So it needs to appeal to your audience whether they're penny pinchers, action-oriented fitness freaks or time-poor business owners. Note that your social personality doesn't necessarily have to *mimic* that of your audience, but should be 'one step ahead' — for example either *more* penny pinching, *more* action oriented or *even* busier.

You wouldn't expect the official Mercedes Twitter account to complain about things like "back to work on Monday morning" for example, whereas a nightclub Twitter account could use this to build affinity and participate in the conversation their customers are already having in their heads: "I can't wait for the weekend and it's only 9:15 am on Monday".

As well as having a clear message and persona, you must seek to understand your market on a deep level. The reality is that after working through your message you'll likely have been thinking about your market simultaneously. Whether your target audience is a very narrow sector ('mums of children with wheat allergies' for example) or very broad ('people who buy cheap clothes'), your campaign clearly needs to appeal to the largest possible portion of your audience.

Trouble identifying or defining a market can be symptomatic of a general lack of marketing focus, and this step can sometimes prove difficult for businesses that haven't previously considered their marketing message. That's OK and it might require a longer period of study to get this finely tuned. This work can be some of the most profitable work you do, and corners shouldn't be cut in any step that involves building affinity and understanding your audience. At the same time, remember that you don't have to get it *perfect*; you just have to get it *going*. You can always adjust your course along the way.

Some questions to ask if you want to make sure that you *truly* understand your audience:

- What is their greatest fear or worry?
- What keeps them awake at night?
- What discussions are they having with their spouse or partner?
- What really drives them?
- What does their typical day look like? The narrower you can focus, the better: when do

they get up? What is the first thing they do when they get to work?

- How do they perceive you and others in your industry?
- What's the preconception about your product or service? Why?

While some of these questions might seem trivial, they all help to build a really clear customer avatar in your mind. Once you have this ideal customer in mind, your marketing becomes much easier because it feels like planning a message to one person rather than a wide diverse group of people you have little affinity with.

The third planning step is to identify your method of communication, or how and where you will communicate to your audience. Each social network has a different user profile and sharing habits. The chances are that if you have similar interests to your audience you'll already have some ideas for the most relevant social networks for your business. If you don't have this insight, my recommendation would be to start doing as much as you can across Facebook and Twitter to begin with, and see what drives the highest engagement with your audience.

Again it's important not to get caught up in the planning to the extent that actually *doing stuff* gets put off until a day in the future that never arrives. If in doubt, *do it.*

It's also worth mentioning that if you are really tuned to your audience or business, many of the points covered above will seem really intuitive and you won't have to invest much time into the planning stage. That's OK too — everyone is different and if you already know where, for whom and how your social media campaign needs to be, power to you. Hit the ground running and let's get going!

Day To Day Social Media Management

Managing your social media campaign doesn't need to be a time vampire as long as you are effective, goal-oriented and stick to the plan. The 'always on' nature and constant refreshing does mean that it's possible to spend all your time being *busy* instead of *productive*, so it's important to clearly differentiate business social media time from personal social media time.

What we usually recommend is putting aside some time each week to plan the following week's content. This allows you to get completely 'in the zone' and create or source content, write the status updates and time them to go out across the week using Buffer or Hootsuite. If you see anything during the course of the week that warrants a Tweet or post, you can either bookmark it for next week's plan, or send it out as and when. You might choose to set up notifications or

IFTTT recipes for replies and messages, depending on how many you get and the urgency of your particular business. But having social media applications running in the background all day long constantly popping up and notifying you is a fast way to get into some unproductive habits.

To keep your distraction levels to a minimum you can check social media on breaks, during lunch and in a dedicated 'interaction' time each day.

DIY Social Media vs. Outsourcing

The decision of whether to run your social media campaign yourself or outsource it is an important one. Generally we recommend that if you *want* to do it yourself that probably means you should at least give it a go.

Some people will read this book, like the sound of what is mentioned but won't like the idea of having to do the work themselves, monitor progress and adjust course accordingly. For those people, finding someone to take care of the social media accounts on their behalf is a good idea.

Others will have the best intentions, but the reality is that once 'real life' kicks in and they are in the day to day of their business, they just won't find the time and their social media campaign will die out slowly.

If you've decided that you'd like to try social media as part of your marketing mix, it's important to be realistic about how you are going to manage this. If you do decide to outsource your social media, we can help manage your campaign. Whether you simply want content curation and timed posts set up each week, or you're looking for a more in-depth help with writing blog posts, doing outreach and managing paid ads, get in touch for your free marketing review and we will be happy to discuss your project and make suggestions for how we can help.

If you decide to outsource your social media elsewhere, here are some tips for choosing a provider:

- Make sure that whomever you choose understands the cultural norms in your country. A lot of outsourced social media profiles are *clearly* outsourced because the character behind the profile makes no attempt at rapport with responders. It comes across like a tiger in a gazelle costume trying to 'blend in'.
- Of course this doesn't mean you are restricted to using social media managers in your own country. Sometimes the best people don't live in your country, and the very best are able to adapt to different cultures and societies and this gives them an edge. Our social media team is spread throughout Europe and the US, and has a wealth of experience from some of the world's

top agencies before they decided to take it to the next level and become Ninajs.

- Make sure that your social media partner makes an effort to understand your business. There is nothing worse than a generic social profile that makes no attempt to demonstrate expertise at all. It comes across as fake and misses the point with your audience, who are looking for you to be an authority. In general, this is often the difference between a 'good value' social media manager and one that is simply cheap. There is already enough information in the world without the need for blasting out social media messages with no additional value being added.
- Be clear about what is and isn't covered in your plan. Some outsourcers will take care of conversations with other users while others won't. Whether you decide that having someone interact with customers is a good thing or not usually depends on the level of technical complexity in your market. Doctors and dentists probably don't want someone answering patient questions on their behalf, whereas a bakery being asked questions about opening times might be glad to be relieved of having to answer such basic queries. Likewise if you want to promote original content in your campaign but you don't have the time to create this content, finding a team who have a writer

on board can save you a lot of time and allow the to get on with it while you're busy running the business.

- The cheapest is not always the best value. This is especially true in marketing. Measure the numbers that are important to you (probably ROI) rather than cost. All that matters to your business is the money that social media brings in compared to what it costs. It makes no sense to artificially restrict social media budget if spending just a little more could bring in a multiple of the return. Of course you don't want to go crazy and break the bank, but pinching pennies in marketing generally shows a focus on the wrong thing — the cost — rather than the true goal — the return.
- Be wary of guarantees. Just like SEO, you'll find social media companies who are more than happy to guarantee results whether it's number of followers, increases in leads or any other metric. While it's great to be confident in one's ability to generate results, this sort of guarantee is based in an environment that they can't control and assumptions that might well prove to be erroneous. So a guarantee is usually either a sign of over optimism about 'knowing it all' or a sign that they'll do anything to make the sale. Fake followers, bought traffic, phony Retweets — any metric can be gamed, so paying based on metrics is not quite as safe a

bet as it might seem. Fake followers destroy your metrics and they're tough to weed out, so you're best off steering clear in the first place.

- Have realistic timescales in mind. Social media marketing is not as immediate as running an ad, getting significant press coverage or other transient advertising methods. If you are down to your last $100 and need customers *this week* in order to keep the lights on, there are other places you should spend that money. But if you are looking for a sustainable long-term way to generate new leads and boost sales from existing leads, social media can be a really useful component of your marketing mix.
- Have realistic expectations. Some businesses come to us expecting that top Google ranking or high social media engagement in their town or industry is the key that unlocks unlimited riches. Improvement is not enough — they want nothing short of utter transformation. But while this sort of exposure tends to be very profitable, it is not a silver bullet and increased exposure doesn't compensate for unclear marketing messages, uncompetitive offerings or an absence of any reason to buy. Social media marketing is one tool in your toolbox, and a handy man with only one tool isn't that handy. Make sure you are putting time into the other areas of marketing your business too. See our website and other books for more information.

- Be realistic about how you'll work. Generally we find clients extremely enthusiastic to be involved in their social activity early on. Once the novelty has worn off they lose interest and the content gets more and more sporadic. If you need a manager who will be on at you every week requesting new bits of news, make sure that's what you're getting. Being effective in this situation isn't about being perfect and having no weaknesses, but understanding how you work, being realistic about your weaknesses and being honest about what it'll take to keep this thing going.
- Be wary of contracts. While it obviously takes time for the effects of any campaign to bear fruit, you will be able to see within a couple months how effective your outsourced social media manager is. Most offer a monthly report showing the progress that is being made, so you'll have information to hand to help you decide how effective they are. Companies that work with minimum term contracts should be treated with caution as the last thing you want is to be locked into a period of working with someone who is ineffective (or worse) and forced to pay the remaining fees just to get out. We see no reason for contracts as if both parties are happy with the work being done; the relationship should continue trouble free. If the

client is unhappy for any reason, they should be free to go with no argument or fuss.

Next Steps

If you like what you've seen in this book, remember that we are here to answer any questions you might have. We'd also be happy to offer you a completely free of charge website and marketing review — whether or not you already have social profiles set up. This review will take a look at your existing positioning and make some suggestions about how you can use your website and social media to position your business in your market.

To claim your free audit, head to http://www.exposureninja.com/review

I really hope you've enjoyed reading this book as much as we enjoyed putting it together for you. If you have any comments, suggestions or feedback you can contact me directly tim@exposureninja.com

If you're not happy with the book in any way, I'd also like to know. I'd be happy to personally refund you the cost of the book if you don't consider it a good investment. Just drop me an email and we'll get it sorted :-)